Maddy

5-13-65

(62-13719)

A NEW RUSSIA?

By Harrison E. Salisbury

Fiction

THE NORTHERN PALMYRA AFFAIR

Nonfiction

A NEW RUSSIA?

MOSCOW JOURNAL—THE END OF STALIN

TO MOSCOW—AND BEYOND

THE SHOOK-UP GENERATION

AMERICAN IN RUSSIA

RUSSIA ON THE WAY

A

NEW

RUSSIA?

HARRISON E. SALISBURY

HARPER & ROW, PUBLISHERS
NEW YORK and EVANSTON

For C. and P.

Contents

A NEW RUSSIA?

1. Back to Russia

THE SLEEK ILYUSHIN-18 with its red markings climbed rapidly in the azure sky and below us the high ranges of the Pamirs were powdered with snow that sparkled like sugar crystals in the golden sun. It was mid-November and for the sixth time in eighteen years I was flying into Russia, approaching through the back door of the Asian heartland, the air route from Kabul to Tashkent.

To return to Russia is never a light undertaking but this time I was going back with a deep, almost visceral sense of apprehension.

Just two months previously, in early September, 1961, I had been strolling down a quiet Vermont road with a friend who like myself had spent many years in Russia and much time and energy trying to puzzle out the Soviet enigma. On that afternoon, too, the sun had been golden and the skies a deep and cloudless blue. The pines and spruce up toward Smugglers Notch stood almost black against the old granite hills and here and there a maple had been prematurely touched with fire. We paused a moment beside a clear stream that tumbled down among the boulders.

My friend broke the silence.

"I have never felt this way before," he said. "But it seems to me that there is a real chance that—within the next two or three weeks—Russia and ourselves could be at war."

I nodded my head. So it seemed to me, too, and so it seemed to many of the scientists who were gathered at Stowe that week to discuss in this peaceful old American setting the suicidal problems of war and peace with which man's technological genius and political ineptitude had suddenly confronted the world. There were at Stowe many of the very men whose brilliance had contributed toward the catastrophe which now loomed.

Here were the physicists of America, of Russia, of England, France and many other countries, who had built the nuclear weapons and devised methods of sending them by rocket to any portion of the globe. Here were men who had mastered the mysteries of outer space and others who were on the verge of plumbing the secrets of the life process itself.

And in the councils of these great minds there was an atmosphere of gloom. They better than almost any other men knew the nature of the Pandora's box which their ingenuity had opened. It would not be fair to say that they had given up hope of averting disaster (this was just at the moment when Russia had announced the resumption of nuclear testing and no one knew what the next fateful step might be), but their hopes were based more on faith and habit than on scientific rationale.

To talk with the physicists of Russia and the United States in those September days was to feel the hot draft from the fiery furnace of world incandescence touching the back of your neck. It was so close you could almost taste it.

Now two months and a little more had passed. Inch by inch we had pulled back from the brink. It was clear that for this time, at least, we had, by one means or another, been spared from nuclear suicide. During most of this time I had been traveling through ancient lands—Iran and Afghanistan —so remote from the modern world that they were little aware of the peril in which they had been living. In the deserts of the Khuzistan or the mountains north of Kabul men are too preoccupied in the daily struggle for survival against hunger, cold, trachoma or tuberculosis to worry over fallout or thermonuclear blast even if they could understand what the words mean.

But on this bright November day I was flying back into the Soviet Union, over the high Pamirs and the spurs of the Hindu Kush, over the ancient Amu Darya—the Oxus of classical times—where on one side ragged Afghans, barefoot and often hungry, look across the swift-flowing stream to the columns of Russian trucks which each day convoy the Tajik and Uzbek workers to the neat, irrigated fields of the collective and state farms that lie along the Russian side of the frontier with Afghanistan.

I was returning to the Soviet Union once again to assess that complex and difficult land, to try to measure the deep currents of popular mood and feeling, to talk once more with her leadership group and try to venture some conclusions as to the forces which motivated it, to mingle with the people and share with them their hopes and aspirations, to get some new idea of Russian progress in the endless and infinite task of building up the country and raising its standard of living, to probe again into the security-shrouded riddle of relations between Moscow and Peking, to see for myself how aware Russia might be of the peril which overhung the world and what chance there might be for intelligent steps toward greater international security and, not least, to scan the horizon for signs of basic change which might yield clues to the direction in which Soviet society was likely to evolve.

But my mood was hardly optimistic as I joined the crowd of Afghans and Russians boarding the neat Ilyushin at the Kabul Airport. After months of deep international crisis it seemed only reasonable to suppose that the freeze would be on in Russia so far as contact between Russians and foreigners was concerned—and particularly with American journalists. I had lived through deep-freeze periods in the past. In the last years of the Stalin regime I had often walked the streets of Moscow all day long, like an invisible man, a ghost in a city surrounded by five million Russians, not one of whom spoke to me for hours on end. Those were the days when Russians, spotting a foreigner's clothing, gave him leeway on the sidewalk, when old friends walked past you with blind, staring eyes, when almost the only human contact was the clumsy approach of the *agent provocateur* or the innocent question of the country peasant who mistook you for a Moscow citizen of "culture."

Was this the kind of Russia to which I was returning? It seemed more than likely. Small chance that the atmosphere of my trip in the summer of 1959, the summer of the American Exposition in Moscow, the Nixon visit to Russia and the Khrushchev trip to America, had survived the hot blasts of 1961. By now the omnipresent Soviet security forces would be gaining the upper hand. Once again I would see the furtive look over the shoulder, hear the hushed voice lest someone be eavesdropping, and see on Russian faces the unmistakable marks of fear.

I had been intrigued by the sidewalk forums of 1959, the knots of Russians which surrounded Americans outside their

[4]

hotels, indulging in free-for-all talk of democracy and Communism. I had been amazed by the eagerness of Russian students, tagging me down Gorky Street to practice English. But what most impressed me had been the confidence with which Russians now talked amongst themselves. No longer did fear of the informer, terror of midnight arrest and the concentration camp color every Russian's relations with his countrymen. As a friend expressed it: "It isn't that Russians no longer fear talking with foreigners. They no longer are afraid of each other. That is what is important."

For the first time in thirty years Russians felt secure enough to begin to trust—rather than fear—contacts with each other. Stalin's terror had begun to fade. It had been replaced with confidence that the country was moving toward a regime of law and order in which arbitrary arrest and execution no longer was the commonplace of life. True, there were many skeptics. Many persons had been branded so deeply by horror that they took no chances. And, of course, the police still existed. They could make their comeback, as over Russia's long history they had time and again.

If—as I thought—the chill was on again in Russia, the young and lightly rooted flowers of liberalism would be the first to perish. The hatchetmen of the Stalin era would be on the loose. I had seen enough in those copies of *Pravda* which had come into my hands and had heard enough from Soviet officials to be prepared for severe retrogression from the high-water mark of relaxation which I had found in 1959.

Indeed, even my return to the Soviet Union this time had been marked by difficulties, delays and numerous signs that the friendly professional contacts which had sprung up between American and Soviet newsmen over the past two years were quickly withering in the tensions of the renewed Soviet-American crisis. I might be mistaken, but it seemed reasonable

[5]

to suppose that I would find ordinary Russians distant—if not hostile. Official Russians probably would be correct—but antagonistic. My Soviet newspaper colleagues would, I expected, give me a quick handshake and a sharp word. And my personal friends in Russia would deftly indicate to me that it would be better if we did not meet.

These were some of my thoughts as I unbuckled my seat belt and looked about the comfortable Ilyushin. Just ahead of me sat a beautiful, young, blond, slender Russian girl with a great fat baby boy in bright blue velveteen dress who seemed almost as big as herself and considerably bigger than her small dark husband with the studious hallmarks of the Soviet intellectual who sat proudly beside her. Most of the passengers looked like Soviet engineers, hearty, robust men, returning from work on assistance projects in Afghanistan or Afghan businessmen, taking advantage of the cheap Aeroflot fares to fly to Europe by way of Moscow.

There were no clues to be sensed from this nondescript crowd as to what might lie ahead. The Aeroflot stewardess, like so many of her sisters, was a stern taskmistress who passed out little candies and Soviet journals like a bored teacher humoring dull students at the end of a long day.

Just after the sun had sunk in a blaze of crimson and purple we swung over Tashkent, more sprawling than ever in the gathering autumn dusk. It looked busy and business-like and if it seemed ill lit beside the blazing spectacle of its nearest big neighbor of the non-Communist world, Teheran, the glow and smoke of Tashkent industry let you know that you were descending upon an Asian Pittsburgh rather than an Asian Hollywood.

Hardly had the plane touched down when it was boarded by white-robed doctors and nurses, carrying kettles full of thermometers, almost as big as those used by veterinarians.

They passed down the aisle popping one between the gaping jaws of every passenger. For five minutes . . . ten . . . fifteen we sat waiting for our temperatures to be taken (a procedure introduced because of outbreaks of smallpox and cholera in Asian countries to the south and east). Then, with a smile, the thermometers were quickly collected and read and once more I stepped down onto Russian soil. There was snow on the ground and a cold wind. It felt like Russia, not like Central Asia.

The customs officials were pleasant and efficient. My bags were waved through. The border control officer apologized for making me wait a few minutes while he stamped my passport. The Intourist representative seemed friendly and light-hearted. "My name is Bach," he said with a flourish. I said this did not sound like a Russian name. No, he agreed, "I am an Uzbek." I said it didn't sound Uzbek either. He looked at me quizzically. "You know something about Russia, perhaps?" he asked. I admitted that I did. The young man laughed jovially.

"Well," he said, "my name is really Bakhtiar but you know no foreigner is ever going to be able to remember that. So I just tell people my name is Bach. It makes them feel more at home."

We rode into town through streets lighted with slant-angled neon lights not much different from those of the United States. I had visited Tashkent twice previously, most recently only seven or eight years ago. But there were great patches of the city which I did not recognize, transformed as they were from ancient Asian mud hovels to areas of apartment houses. There was a new modernistic railroad station to replace the sooty train shed where I first took the train to Samarkand in wartime days, new factories, new movie houses and in the great central square before the Navoi Opera

House a huge new hotel in a faithful imitation of the grandiose architecture which Stalin's bad taste made standard.

The lights of the Navoi Opera House were blazing. Above it shone out an electric banner proclaiming the victories of Communism. The great square was alive with people streaming back and forth between the opera and the hotel. Inside the hotel hundreds of persons were milling about, many of them with the bluff, big-shouldered appearance of the provincial party functionary.

"What's up?" I asked my friend Bach.

"Khrushchev's here," he said. "They've just wound up a big three-day agriculture meeting at the Opera House. As you see—everybody's in town."

And so they were. Khrushchev, it appeared, had just made his exit but the hotel swarmed with party secretaries, newspapermen, local functionaries, collective farm chairmen, honored hog growers, medal-bedecked milkmaids, Russians, Uzbeks, Kazaks, Tajiks. It was like state fair week in Des Moines, the night the political candidates have made their appearance. The dining room roared with conversation and the clink of glasses. Delegates hurried to and fro, their arms laden with packages bought at the special store, specially stocked and specially opened "For Delegates Only" on the second-floor mezzanine.

If a deep freeze had clamped down on Russian life I saw little sign of it. No one frowned at me. When I took a vacant seat at a table the Russians asked me where I came from. When I said "America" they did not slink away. Nor did they bombard me with questions. They hoped I had had a good trip, that I did not mind the cold and asked what the weather was like in New York. Then they went back to talking about increasing the cotton yields on their irrigated lands.

In the third-floor lobby of the hotel there was a TV set

and I stopped to watch for a while before going to bed. A dozen men and women, enthralled by a second-rate comedy about collective farm life, watched silently, very much like groups I had seen a dozen times sitting around the TV set in hotels in Moline, Illinois, or Fresno, California. The only real difference was the absence of commercials and the smaller picture tube. After the movie finished I talked a bit with my neighbors and then retired to my room to sort out my impressions. There was an ease which was at variance with the tension I had expected to find. There had not been a single reference to "American warmongers" and no mention of the war which *Pravda* so often talked of. Perhaps this was because I was in the provinces of Central Asia, far from Moscow. A few years previously the appearance of an American in this milieu would have caused a sensation. Tonight I had met friendly curiosity, but no excitement. Clearly, there was a growing sophistication in the provinces. Foreigners were no longer the rarity they had been.

And all about there was other evidence of change—the TV set, the hotel itself, the new street lighting, the new buildings, better clothing (the tie and the white shirt, I saw, had finally conquered the Russian male). The food was good, the borsch rich and swimming with oil.

First impressions sometimes play you false but, unless I was badly mistaken, Russia—by Russian standards—was living quite well and the telltale signs of tension and restriction were absent. Two years earlier the most striking fact about life inside Russia was the pace at which relaxation had proceeded and the stimulation it had given to the natural forces of free inquiry, philosophical challenge and political skepticism. I had long observed that in Russia the social process is governed by geometric law. The reaction in the province is in inverse proportion to the distance from the center—

Moscow. If I found in the heart of Central Asia a measurable improvement in Russian living standards and an obvious liberalization, I should find even stronger evidence of these tendencies in the Soviet capital. A trip to Russia is always a journey of discovery and it seemed that surprises awaited me. If Russia had been able to endure five months of sharpening world tension without reaching for the lever marked "police"; if not even the threat of war had touched off a major regression from the freer tendencies so evident two years ago; if the xenophobic currents which lie close to the Russian surface had not again been stimulated; if modest but measurable improvement in everyday living had continued; it seemed possible that Russia might be able to make a contribution to the stability of the world greater than anyone expected. But all of this, of course, presupposed a political and social maturity considerably more advanced than I or most Western observers believed had been achieved in the nearly nine years since Stalin's death.

I had been absent from Russia only twenty-six months and I had spent much of the intervening period in close contact with Russian missions to the United States—the two trips of Premier Khrushchev, the visits of cultural artists, the frequent forays of Soviet journalists.

Was it possible so easily to miss the tempo of Russian evolution? Or were my first impressions of Tashkent distorted by subjective expectations of a new "deep freeze"? Clearly, I thought, as I clambered into the Ukrainian bed with its lacy cover and mountain of pillows, the Russian puzzle grows more fascinating and intricate with each new crisis, each passing year.

The fate of the world did not, of course, depend on whether people frowned or smiled in a distant million-peopled city of Central Asia; the question of survival in an age threatened by nuclear suicide did not hinge on how the guests of a Tashkent hotel greeted a chance visitor from America. And yet these were not the kind of clues which anyone studying the Soviet enigma would lightly dismiss. Because if Premier Khrushchev and his associates had set their course firmly toward collision, the first signs of such a decision would appear inside and not outside the country. In no nation is internal policy more closely linked to external. If the Kremlin really expected that the international crisis would lead to war, the tightening up on the home front would be in full swing by now.

My stay in Russia would not be long—probably only a couple of months. I would have to economize my time, concentrating on those areas of Soviet life most sensitive to change—youth, the intelligentsia, the writers and poets, minority groups like the Jews, the Orthodox Church. I must try to learn who was moving upward in the power pyramid and what had been the repercussions of the new denunciations of Stalin. And, if possible, I must try once more to visit Outer Mongolia and reassess the deepening conflict between Moscow and Peking, which might, after all, prove the most important factor in the whole complicated and dangerous problem.

Only too often, as I well knew, in the fast rush of day-by-day events we lost from view those tidal movements in the continental Russian masses which in the end must prove decisive in determining the course of history and, quite possibly, the fate of our age.

2. The "Lost Generation"

THE PLAY at the Samarkand Drama Theater was bad and the theater cold and uncomfortable. The play dealt with an American scientist who sells out to the warmongers and is sent to Hawaii to work on a new kind of space weapon. Its high spot was a hula dance, performed by several nice blond Ukrainian girls, garbed in bikinis, goose-pimples and embarrassment. I had never seen anything so undressed and so gauche on the Russian stage but the audience, largely girls in their late teens and early twenties, seemed to enjoy the spectacle.

At the interval I fell into conversation with a bright-eyed, well-groomed youngster of twenty-one. How did she like the play? She wrinkled her snub nose quizzically.

"Of course," she said, "you must realize that this is just a provincial theater. But the play is very interesting to us. The background is so exotic and strange."

She hoped that I did not take amiss the anti-American content of the play (since the propaganda was directed against U.S. testing of nuclear weapons at a moment when the Russians, rather than the Americans, had broken the test ban, the whole play had really been turned topsy-turvy) and made no secret of her delight at a chance to talk with an American. Her deepest ambition, she explained, was to travel. She had been born and brought up in a big Volga River town and after graduating from the university had asked to be sent to teach school in Samarkand "because at least Central Asia is different."

Now she had spent a year there and found that life was only too similar to that of her Volga town.

"I must go abroad," she said. "I must! Even if only to Rumania. If you only knew how boring life is in Russia!"

I sensed the lament of a whole generation in this young girl's remark. In one form or another, as I was so often told, life in Russia seemed to them "so boring." This was their central concern—not international politics, not the world revolution, certainly not Communist doctrine, or even questions of war or peace. And they displayed not the slightest backwardness in expressing themselves freely and even vehemently to a foreigner. No sign of a chill here. If the Kremlin was preparing for war the youngsters did not show it.

These young people, raised entirely under Communism, never having known anything but a Marxist environment, barely old enough to remember World War II and Stalin, had become, I quickly found, the despair of the Communist party.

"This is our greatest defeat," a middle-aged, serious Communist party official said to me later in Moscow. "The young people have deserted the cause. I do not know how we are going to get them back."

The alienation of the young people took many forms. I

[13]

saw it in the boredom and restlessness of young girls in Central Asia. In the drunkenness which persisted in eastern Siberia. In the hooliganism of Moscow restaurants. And in the cool disdain of the generation of indifference, the well-educated, cultured young people, sons and daughters of high party or government officials, who had a Western counterpart in the habitués of San Francisco's hungry i, the pads of Greenwich Village or the cafés of the Boulevard St. Germain.

I had seen the stirrings of Soviet youth in 1959—the emergence of the *stilyagi,* or "stylish ones," with their zoot suits, dog-chain watch fobs, floppy trousers and Tarzan haircuts. But I was hardly prepared two years later to discover that discontent had permeated the whole age group, fifteen to twenty-five. Not that all Soviet youth had gone nihilistic. Far from it. Out in eastern Siberia I was to find young men and women, brimming with energy and enthusiasm, working in 40 degree below zero cold, pouring concrete for great dams, erecting steel for factories, installing machinery in temperatures so frigid they could work not more than ten minutes of the hour, spending the rest of the time thawing their frozen hands over coal oil stoves. The youngsters, mobilized by the Communist Youth, were laboring to complete the Bratsk dam on the Angara, the largest in the world, the huge Shelekhov Aluminum complex near Irkutsk and even bigger projects at Krasnoyarsk on the Yenisei. Not all these young people were happy. But among the forty thousand at Bratsk enthusiasm seemed more common than disaffection. And at Moscow University our American students found no lack of tough, argumentative, young party red-hots with whom to debate the relative merits of democracy and socialism.

To me the dramatic fact about life in the Union of

Soviet Socialist Republics in the forty-fifth year after the Bolshevik Revolution was not that there still existed cadres of young people who supported the regime but that right across the grain of Soviet society from the dark provinces beyond the Volga to the neon lights of Moscow's Gorky Street (which the youngsters persisted in calling Brodvai) symptoms of dissatisfaction were to be seen at every hand.

No wonder the Communist party was at wit's end as to how to deal with the situation. Its reaction often resembled that of the civic elders in an American town, plagued by an outburst of adolescent delinquency. The Communists reached for the nightstick as quickly as their counterparts in the U.S.A. I was constantly reading editorials and letters in the Soviet press demanding sterner action against youthful offenders.

One winter's day as I walked down Gorky Street I saw a crowd around a window at Pushkin Square. Photographs of young people accused of being idlers were on display under the legend: "Parasites! Get Out!"

"That's right!" a stern-visaged, middle-aged woman said to her neighbor in the crowd. "They should put up their pictures. Something must be done with these young wastrels."

I saw approving nods among the spectators, many of whom were obviously out-of-town visitors. Two young men on the edge of the crowd exchanged winks. As they moved down the street I noticed that they were wearing "Texas trousers"— blue jeans, possibly the most prized status symbol of the "Lost Generation," and the one which most infuriated the party propagandists.

As *Komsomolskaya Pravda,* the Youth paper noted, the blue denim from which "Texas trousers" are made is not even produced in the Soviet Union. It is a fabric unknown in Soviet life. Where do the Texas trousers come from? They are smuggled into Russia, probably from Poland or East Germany.

At the Kiev railroad station in Moscow I saw posters in the waiting room which read: "You shall not pass. We have no place for hooligans in our society."

But a few nights before while standing in a queue near the post office waiting for a taxicab—for some reason Moscow's taxis, once numerous, seem to vanish from the streets during the five o'clock and after-theater rush hours—a vicious fist fight broke out which was halted only when passers-by called the police. A drunken youth had committed a public nuisance which the escort of a well-dressed woman very properly resented. A little later I watched two hopelessly drunken young men stagger past my hotel, stumbling into pedestrians, cursing freely in what the Russians call *"mat"*—or "mother oaths," the most vulgar profanity.

Not long thereafter I was dining in the Budapest Restaurant. A few years ago this was called the Peking Restaurant and before that the Aurora. The menu changed little with each change of name and the character of the restaurant even less. It was a rather loud, brassy place with a big orchestra which attracted Moscow young people with money to spend.

On this particular night there was a party of about twenty young men, muscular fellows, obviously members of a sports team. They were drinking and, as is often the case, they were mixing champagne, vodka and brandy in fairly equal amounts. A dark-haired young man with a pretty blond girl danced near the celebrants. Suddenly, I saw the girl's escort and one of the athletes scuffling. Someone separated them and the boy and girl went to a table across the room. A few minutes later the drunken athlete bounded from his chair, dashed over and attacked the young man. The girl was knocked to the floor, and when she was picked up, blood ran from her nose and mouth.

A moment later the hooligan rejoined his companions. A few heads were turned, there was a buzz of conversation, but the incident was so routine that the waiters didn't even stop their service to intervene.

In the provinces the brawling took a more serious character. And the same, I was told, could be said of Moscow's sprawling industrial suburbs. There the young toughs organized like the "bopping" clubs of Brooklyn or the street gangs which more than a century ago reigned supreme in some New York areas where police ventured only at the peril of their lives.

I could hardly pick up the paper without reading that bands of hooligans were terrorizing the good citizens of Pskov or Saratov or Zagorsk. A favorite target seemed to be police officers and even police stations. Sometimes, the police were murdered and the station houses burned down. What the Young Communist propagandists liked to call the "bacilli" of hooliganism seemed to have spread throughout the Soviet body politic.

For more than three years the Communist party had been conducting a campaign against youthful violence. They launched their drive after a spectacular murder in Leningrad of a Moscow Komsomol named Vadim Trainin, knifed to death by a young man he was trying to arrest. Trainin's brutal murder was utilized to kick off a national propaganda drive. The *druzhina,* a volunteer auxiliary police force made up of squads of Communist Youth, was organized to patrol the streets, seeking to dissuade young people from drinking too much. They were supposed to help the regular police preserve public order, particularly in cafés, restaurants, clubs and dance halls.

The sale of strong drink was curbed. Western-style bars were abolished. Mr. Khrushchev himself set a national example by eschewing vodka and restaurants were ordered to limit vodka sales to one drink per customer. But I could see few positive results. The druzhina, as might have been expected, had become bureaucratized. Most of those I saw on the streets were not young people but retired army officers who plodded about, bored and disinterested. They had acquired snug little command posts and were little more than an inefficient arm of the police.

In many provincial cities, the papers complained, the druzhina had simply disappeared. In other towns they were the first to take cover when a brawl was brewing.

The cafés and restaurants which I visited made mockery of the government's temperance drive. They limited sales of vodka (except for what they sold under the counter) but they eagerly sold brandy by the bottle at a price about 50 percent above that charged for vodka. And they sold unlimited quantities of fortified 40-proof sherry to anyone who came along. If a young man wanted to order a drink of vodka, two bottles of wine and a bottle of brandy, they were glad to oblige—so long as he had the rubles to pay.

Drunkenness had been characteristic of Russia for so many centuries that I doubted that it particularly alarmed the Soviet authorities. The root of their concern lay in the anti-regime, antagonistic, nihilistic moods which emerged when Russian young people began to drink heavily.

The authorities were invoking more and more severe penalties. The death sentence—against which traditionally there had been deep prejudice in Russia—was introduced against "persistent hooliganism" in 1961. And by 1962 it had been extended to cover a broad series of offenses, characteristic of adolescent delinquency, such as attacks upon police officers, volunteer public order patrols, government officials, etc.

There could be little doubt that the widening use of the death penalty reflected the frustration of Soviet authorities at their inability to create a generation of young people bearing any resemblance to the word picture of Communist youth which they had painted for themselves and the world at large.

I was surprised in the summer of 1959 to find loitering openly near the principal Moscow and Leningrad hotels English-speaking young men who approached tourists with offers to exchange rubles for dollars at very favorable rates, to sell ancient icons at bargain prices or to purchase American sports shirts for the equivalent of $40 or $50.

In my long years in Russia I had never seen open currency speculation and black marketing in the streets. Now it was being carried on by well-dressed, well-educated, self-confident young men. The uniformed police paid them no heed. Neither did the plain-clothes details which, even in the Khrushchev era, clustered around the hotel areas.

I could only conclude that the young men were operating with the connivance of the secret police. This impression was strengthened when I learned that some of the "biznesmen," as they called themselves, had been arrested and then turned loose to continue their activities. It was my guess that the secret police had a hand in the currency trade (as they had often had on past occasions) and that, perhaps, they needed additional dollars for their far-flung undercover operations in other countries.

What I found most ironic about this situation was the fact that open speculation by young people in Moscow dated from the convening of the big World Youth Festival which the Russians held in the summer of 1957— an event which had been marked by great relaxation of all kinds of normal restrictions. The chief public legacy of this international propaganda fete had turned out to be a currency racket in which enterprising young Muscovites and the notorious secret police appeared to be partners.

The currency dealing went forward with no interference until after the introduction of the new "hard" ruble in 1961. This established the value of the ruble at $1.11. In the accompanying adjustment of prices the exchange value of the ruble and the dollar for the first time in years was fixed on a fairly realistic basis.

Hardly had the new value been set when the police "discovered" the currency racket. The operators in Moscow were suddenly arrested. With great fanfare it was revealed that they had dealt in millions of dollars through a network that extended all over the country. Some members collected rare icons in Siberia, stealing them from churches for sale to foreigners. Others were located in Georgia. They had great hoards, it was said, of gold and jewels. Just where the gold and jewels came from was a little vague.

The principal criminals were put on trial on Moscow not long before I arrived there. They were convicted and sentenced to fifteen years in prison. But, on appeal, a new trial was ordered. This time the three ringleaders were ordered shot under an ex post facto law which had been enacted long after the crimes had been committed.

Since then currency speculators had been ordered shot in Georgia, in the Ukraine and in the Baltic states. The press had given great attention to these crimes. There were a dozen curious circumstances about these cases—not the least of which was whether the police had not shot the operators to cover up their own tracks. But one thing was certain. Currency speculation among Moscow's young people had come to a dead halt. The young people of the beat generation, the shook-up generation or the lost generation—call it what you would—were just as eager as ever before for the bright baubles of the West. But they were not going to risk getting shot for the sake of dollars to buy them with.

This was the only dent, so far as I could see, which the authorities had been able to make in their drive against youthful behavior which violated Communist norms.

In some fields the effort had simply been abandoned. No longer was any attempt being made to hold the line against Western music and jazz. The sound of Western rhythms echoed from every restaurant in Moscow. The cha-cha-cha blared forth on the eastern Siberian radio network. The repertoire of the blond songstress at the Uzbekistan Restaurant in Moscow was mostly American numbers, some of them sung in English. Soviet caricaturists inveighed against rock 'n' roll. Playwrights satirizing the West invariably included a café sequence featuring a bizarre exaggeration of what they called the "boogi-voogi." But Russian young people had left these dances far behind. The vogue today was for the cha-cha-cha, the mambo, the samba, the rumba, Latin rhythms. The bars against these long-prohibited dances had come tumbling down on the theory that they were "Cuban popular folk dances" and, therefore, perfectly admissible.

The strange alliance of Fidel Castro with Moscow had had another effect—it had brought back the beard. The Communist regime shared the distaste of Peter the Great for the beard. Peter with his own scissors snipped off the whiskers of his courtiers as a gesture against Russian backwardness.

The Communists were equally antagonistic toward beards —except for distinguished surgeons and members of the Academy of Science. A beard on a young Russian was equated with fondness for things past, the Orthodox Church and,

perhaps, with dissent. The antipathy of the Communist
Youth movement for hirsute adornment had grown no less.
But beards were sprouting on the chins of young Russians—
fringe beards, scraggly beards, luxuriant naval beards, beat
beards—all the varieties which might be encountered on an
American campus. The urgent recommendations of Young
Communists for use of a razor and lather met the insur-
mountable argument: "Sorry, but Fidel Castro is my hero.
Surely, you do not want to give offense to our Cuban com-
rade."

In the dining room of the National Hotel I found well-
dressed young men with Princeton or Yale haircuts. They
wore suits of dark blue or Oxford gray. Their shirts were
white and their ties neat, narrow, Italian-striped or, sometimes, a thin straight bow of dark silk. Occasionally, they
wore solid-color shirts of dark blue with a contrasting tie of
yellow or powder blue. Their trousers were pencil slim and
they wore well-made Italian black leather pumps. On the
street they sported a kind of porkpie hat with flaring brim
—a little like that which the late Gary Cooper used to
favor—and hip-length, fawn-colored camel's-hair coats.

The girls with these young men did their hair in lovely
blond beehives or other variants of flowing French and
Italian hair-dos. They dressed in well-cut, short cocktail
dresses, often off the shoulder. Their nylons were Western
or high-style Soviet production (costing $5.50 a pair). Many
had Italian spike-heel shoes or fair copies from Czechoslovakia. Some were hand-made by Moscow shoemakers.

Other girls patterned themselves after Brigitte Bardot.
Only one Bardot picture had been shown in Moscow, *Babette
Goes to War,* in which she played a well-clothed girl soldier.
But young people had seen more characteristic pictures of
Bardot in East European magazines. In the Moscow cafés the

How did young people react to them? Out in Siberia one evening at the theater I was surrounded by a group of excited teen-agers. Here is the way the conversation went:

"Have you seen *America Through the Eyes of the French?* What a wonderful picture! Is life in America really so thrilling? Here things are so boring! Do you really have automobile graveyards in America? Are there really teen-age gangs? Do they fight each other? Do you really smash up cars by deliberately running them into each other? [They were referring to a county fair "wreck" sequence.] How much does the cheapest car cost in America—not a new one but an old one? Only $100 or $200? Then, it's really so that young people own their own cars and drive everywhere they want?"

And so on. The whole discussion was carried on in exclamation marks and italics. I talked to older Russians who were depressed or even shocked by some of the sequences in the pictures. But not the youngsters. All they dreamt of was the day when they, too, might have cars and drive where they pleased.

Not only did the "lost generation" often look like its American counterpart, but it talked in a special teen-age slang, comprehensible only to itself and closely resembling the teen-age jargon of America. In fact, some expressions were of Western derivation. The boys called each other "zhentlmen." They peppered their conversation with words like "tip-top" and "okay." Whereas a few years ago they called their girl friends "Zhane" (after Tarzan's Jane), they now called her "Brigitte."

They told each other: "Don't be afraid, lads, keep your pistol in your belt"—a phrase they apparently picked up from old Western films or smuggled-in comic books. Comic

girls appeared with ponytail hair-dos, black cotto
flat-heeled shoes. Their escorts affected fringe bea
tans.

These were the young people who in the win
began to approach foreigners in the restaurants, ;
you know how to do the twist?"

Word of the twist had reached them quick
Moscow papers published blurry photographs c
dance together with vituperative attacks on this li
festation of Western decadence. All the propagan
to stimulate a youthful thirst for the new craze.

This reaction was characteristic. Western styles
tastes, Western dances, Western ways—these were
of Soviet youth. They rushed to the big newsstand o
Square to buy the latest Polish newspapers or the
Communist papers like *L'Unità* of Italy, *L'Hun*
France or the London *Daily Worker*. They carri
around even when they could not read them—as a
status symbol. From these papers they extracte
impressions of how people lived and dressed in th
Non-Communist Western publications still were no
Russia, but young people obtained copies of *Life*, *7
Vogue* from tourists and the State Department's I
language slick-paper monthly, *Amerika,* sold out ir
minutes after it reached the newsstands.

Another source of Westernism was the anti-Western
Youngsters turned these pictures upside down, glo
what they were supposed to despise. Two such p
were being shown at that time. One was a French
mentary, *America Through the Eyes of the French*
other was a Soviet picture, *Multi-Storied America*. N
film was entirely anti-American but they were being
sented for their negative bias.

books were prized even by teen-agers who could not read a word of English.

I made up a list of the kind of slang they used:

Russian	Literal Translation	Slang Meaning
predki	ancestors	parents
kon	chess knight	the old man
khata	peasant cottage	pad
zhelezny	iron	the most, the greatest
kusok	piece	bread (specifically 1,000 old rubles)
chuvok	probably Ukrainian, possibly derived from word meaning castrated ram	punk
chuvika	same	chick
oryol	eagle	wild, way out
zapravlyat	to mix or season	to tell a lie
tachka	wheelbarrow	heap
flesh-royal	royal flush	the most
pizhon	fop	punk
malchishki	street urchins	beats, J D's
milti or *miltami*	derisive diminutive of militia or police	cop, fuzz

What most interested me was what philosophy motivated these young people. What was their attitude toward life? This was what gave the phenomena a social and political significance. At the lowest level it clearly was unformulated nihilism—the same destructive, pointless aggression which I had seen among the teen-age gangs of New York, brutal violence which underscored the vacuity of their lives.

At a slightly higher level it appeared to be undifferentiated hedonism. A Moscow police investigator, writing about the problem, told of cross-examining a young delinquent, arrested in a roundup of speculators. He asked the young man what he wanted in life.

"My golden desire? Well, nobody wants a heart attack. What do I want? Drink . . . restaurants . . . jazz . . . money . . . women . . . a Volga car . . . a country cottage . . . you know, the complete gentlemen's selection."

I was standing beside a cigarette counter in Kiev one day. It was unattended for the moment. A young man picked up a pack of cigarettes and walked away. "But you didn't pay!" his friend exclaimed.

"I know," the thief replied. "I'm just anticipating the arrival of Communism when everything will be free."

"Do I enjoy my work?" another youngster said to me. "Certainly I do. Every first and fifteenth of the month when I get my pay."

Another one said, "We have heard how great life is and of all the sacrifices which have been made to build our society. Now is the time for us to enjoy it."

But there was a higher level of discontent. This I found among young students who told me that their hero was J. D. Salinger, whose *Catcher in the Rye* had recently appeared in translation. They had read John Cheever, also translated, and Saroyan, Faulkner and Sartre. They collected sophisticated jazz records and attended rather poor showings of nonobjective art, conducted almost conspiratorially in the private studios of some of the *avant-garde* painters.

These young people were the object of sensitive study by young Soviet writers, who themselves had been denounced by the Communist party—not entirely without reason—as being members of the lost generation.

One youngster, in a play by Ivan Kupriyanov, described how he felt:

"It's too boring, being one of the orthodox. You can't do this. You must do that. I'm sick of it. Sick of it all. It doesn't take brains to blat out commonplace truths. If I had the power I would forbid bombast for good."

Another youngster, in a scenario by Viktor Rozov which was savagely denounced by party propagandists, retorted to his mother when she upbraided him, saying he should behave better: "Should! Should! I've hardly entered the world and all I hear is: 'You should do this! You should do that! You should . . .' There is nothing whatever that I *should* do."

The boy runs away from his home and his girl friend tries to comfort him, saying, "I understand you. You are offended now. It seems to you that you are the only one in the whole world. The only, only one. It's been that way with me, too. Sometimes, all of a sudden I am so sad . . . so terribly sad. It seems that no one needs you. You even cry. I cry and cry. . . ."

In one play showing in Moscow a party chief shook his head and observed: "I cannot understand our young people. They have some kind of kink. They are growing up without ideals. They have lost them."

But the reply was: "What kind of ideals were they— that they were so easy to lose?"

What happened to these young Soviet people?

Viktor Rozov put these words into the mouth of his young hero:

"Why have people invented colored TV and tape recording? Why do they seek the secret of protein and want to fly to the moon? And from this they create nothing honest, nothing happy?

"I love all that is good. And you are satisfied with both good and bad. That is your habit. What do I dream? My dreams are very beautiful. For example, to exterminate from the earth all self-satisfied dolts, crooks, careerists, time-servers, toadies, double-dealers."

Or, as Kupriyanov described an important Party figure: "You are building Communism in your own private house. You have put your party card into one pocket and your conscience into the other."

It seemed to me that these Soviet writers had exposed the core of the problem. It was the hypocrisy of Communism, the failure of the Soviet to fulfill its expressed ideals, the decadence of the society and its growing contentment with mundane goals which had driven the young people to search for something better—or at least different.

A few—a comparative few—like those I saw in Siberia, had gone east to try to recapture the flaming ideals of Communism's early days in the struggle to build an industrial complex in the frozen taiga. But more Soviet young people were turning to the West in aimless quest for something to replace Soviet stultification.

Like generations of Russians before them they hoped to find a new "truth," more honest, more revealing than that of Moscow.

One January night I sat in a noisy Moscow restaurant. It was an establishment I had known for many years. I first saw it in the cold and hungry days of wartime Moscow. Then there was no band and food, what there was of it, was served on sharply restricted ration cards. There were no young men in the restaurant and few young women. I knew the restaurant later on in the last Stalin years. By this time it was expensive. There was caviar, beefsteak and champagne for those who had the price, and a dispirited band which played polkas, waltzes and Russian folk tunes. It was not uncommon to see poorly dressed girls dancing together or young soldiers clumping about the dance floor a little woodenly, two by two. Later on, after Stalin died, the band got livelier and I sometimes saw tieless, unpressed factory workers trying to twirl about their frizzy-haired, short-skirted partners in what they fondly imagined was jitter-bugging. Tonight the atmosphere was different. The Russians would have said it was more cultured. The orchestra played Western music. During intermissions a tape recording of "Music U.S.A." with English lyrics was switched on. Many of the young people would have looked perfectly at home in New York or Paris. They danced and dressed conservatively. Their taste was good.

As is the Russian custom, a young couple sat down at my table. The girl wore a gamin hair-do and a pretty blue bouffant cocktail dress. The young man wore a dark suit, white shirt and narrow bow tie and for a moment I thought he had on a dinner jacket. They ordered a carafe of brandy, a bottle of lemonade, a plate of apples and oranges, lemon slices, powdered sugar and a box of chocolate bonbons.

They danced quite often but during an interlude we fell to talking.

"We like American music best," the girl said. "Do you know David Brubeck by any chance?"

I was sorry to say that I didn't.

"We've heard there is a new American dance called the twist," the boy said. I said I had heard that, too, but unfortunately did not know how to do it. Both of them looked disappointed. We talked of several things. Finally, the boy said, "I heard a joke that might amuse you since you are an American. You know our slogan—to catch up with and exceed America?"

Yes, I said, I knew the slogan.

"Well, the joke goes like this: Premier Khrushchev makes a speech, announcing that we are going to catch up with

America. After the speech a man comes up and says, 'Comrade Khrushchev, when we catch up with America—can I stay there?' "

It was an old story but I laughed politely. I asked them whether they had heard the story that it was all right to catch up with America but that Russia better not get ahead in the race or we would see the hole in the seat of their trousers. They laughed politely. Obviously, they knew my story as well as I knew theirs.

Someday, the youngsters said, they hoped to go to America and see it with their own eyes.

I said I hoped that would be possible. I only hoped that these young and eager Soviet searchers for a way of life less gray and false than that of their own land would not find the West, too, a disappointment and a disillusionment.

The new generation of young people had started down a road far different from that which their parents had traveled and far different from that which the Communist party had traced out on its map of the future. Neither the young people nor their elders knew just where this road would lead, nor whether by the time the new generation had gone a little further it would be forcibly detoured back to a path paved with didacticism and dialectic.

But it was plain that the tendencies toward dissent and nonconformity which I had seen in 1959 had deepened and broadened despite party exhortations, despite party bullying and despite the sharpening of international tension. This was the kind of thing which might produce long-term changes in the structure of Soviet society, changes of profound consequence to Russia and the world—if we could avoid nuclear disaster.

The young people could tell me what they were against

—the propaganda, the speeches, the slogans, the queues, the boredom. But not many of them understood very well what they were searching for. Perhaps, I thought, I might find the answers on the lips of the poets, the artists and the scientists, the members of Russia's famous intelligentsia.

3. The New "Men of the Sixties"

On FEBRUARY 10, 1837, Alexander Pushkin, Russia's greatest poet, died of wounds inflicted in a duel, deliberately provoked, as is now known, at the instigation of Czar Nicholas I, who sought thus to silence the most eloquent voice of freedom in his land.

On the 125th anniversary of Pushkin's death Anna Akhmatova published a tribute to him in which she spoke of the enemies, the hatred, the "ocean of filth, perfidy, lies, indifference and stupidity" in which Pushkin was immersed during his life. But with his death all this changed.

Very quickly, [she wrote], all the beauties, the great ladies, the mistresses of salons, the members of the nobility began to be called the contemporaries of Pushkin. People spoke of the Pushkin epoch, the Petersburg of Pushkin. In the palace halls where they once danced and gossiped about the poet they now displayed his portrait and preserved his books. Of the great palaces it was said: Here Pushkin was. Or here Pushkin was not. And nothing else was interesting about them.

These were not antiquarian observations by an elderly lady poetess. They were, like so much else which was being said on the Soviet literary scene in 1962, words pregnant with political meaning—a warning, in fact, to Stalin's politico-literary heirs that Russian history and Russian tradition stand on the side of truth and justice.

There were few figures who could more appropriately voice this warning than Madame Akhmatova because the words she spoke about Pushkin could easily have been applied to herself.

One January day in Moscow I received from the State Literary Publishing House a slender volume in white binding and gold lettering, a copy of the selected works of the 73-year-old Akhmatova. It had just been issued in an edition of 50,000 copies (all of which were snapped up in a few hours). The volume was, in a sense, a testimonial to a woman who was still living but who well might, except for her tough fiber and courage, have expired under just such an "ocean of filth, perfidy and lies" as was directed against Pushkin.

Anna Akhmatova's life was spared, but only by a narrow margin. In the late Stalin years the dictator's Leningrad lieutenant, Andrei A. Zhdanov, drove her out of Soviet literary life. She was expelled from the Union of Soviet Writers, barred from writing for Soviet publications and castigated as "half nun, half fornicatress," a woman who divided her interests between the drawing room, the bedroom and the chapel. Her son, a scholar in the Far Eastern field, was shipped to a Siberian labor camp where he lingered until three years after Stalin's death. Madame Akhmatova would have starved to death but for the aid of a few loyal friends.

[33]

Time and truth were on her side—as they were on the side of Pushkin. Zhdanov died and Stalin died but she lived on to see her poetry once more published; to find the literary journals seeking her out; to write new poetry dedicated to the purity of the muses; to compose a prophetic tribute to Alexander the Great, who—while ordering the destruction of Thebes—made sure that the House of Poets was untouched; and to pay homage to another sensitive artist, one who did not survive the Stalin terror, Marina Tsvetaeva.

From the State Literary Publishing House I obtained a second slender volume, this one bound in powder blue. It contained a selection of Marina Tsvetaeva's work, the first to be published in Russia since the early days of the Revolution. Tragedy has long been the handmaiden of poetry in Russia. Pushkin, Lermontov, Esenin, Mayakovsky, Tsvetaeva—the list of martyred poets might be extended indefinitely. Marina Tsvetaeva found the Bolshevik atmosphere stifling. A few years after the Revolution she went into the emigration. She lived in Prague and then in Paris, but as time passed her yearning for the white birches and green forests became unbearable and she returned on the eve of World War II, only to perish by her own hand in a dirty little Urals village, unable to endure the privation and loneliness of exile within her homeland. Her death went unnoticed, unrecorded in the catastrophe of war and the ice-bound years of Stalin's repression that followed.

Now, twenty years later, the courageous survivors of those years of horror were painstakingly setting the record straight.

And they were doing more. It was not only, I found, that the older generation of survivors like Akhmatova, Paustovsky, Tvardovsky, Ehrenburg and even Simonov were preoccupying themselves with the rectification of past wrongs, with memorial essays and memorial volumes to those who perished in the 1920's, the 1930's and the 1940's in successive waves of hysteria which swept the Stalin regime. It was not only that a man like Ehrenburg had set about to write volume after volume of memoirs in which he called the roll of forgotten and vilified names, going back to the last days of the imperial reign and carrying the account forward right into the present. Not merely this—although this was important enough. No. What I found most impressive as I talked to writers and poets, as I went to the Moscow theaters, as I watched the new issues of literary journals being snapped up like five-star finals at the kiosks and as I read the confused and often contradictory speeches being made by the harassed hacks of the Party propaganda bureau was something much more profound and, it seemed to me, more pregnant with meaning for Russia's future.

What was emerging in the writing of the gifted members of the surviving generation of the older literati was the pure line of the great Russian heritage—the line that went back to the classics of the nineteenth century, the century when Russia's best minds were preparing the way, so they thought, for liberty, democracy and freedom of thought to replace the tyranny, autocracy and shackled ignorance of a decadent empire. The ideals which they preached were those of Pushkin, Tolstoy, Chekhov and Blok, of Herzen, Chernyshevsky and Belinsky.

Nor were the eyes of the older generation fixed on the past. They preached the ideals of the past, they sought to rectify the injustices of the past. But their thoughts were for the present and for the future. Ehrenburg was devoting himself to a re-examination of writers like Stendhal and Chekhov, but not as a literary exercise. He was demonstrating to the young writers of his country the nature of the writer's creed, the sanctity of truth, the inviolability of personality, the incompatibility of patriotism and hypocrisy. He sought out young poets who were picking a path through the brambles of dialectic criticism and encouraged them to be true, first and above all, to their own standards.

Tvardovsky, a man of solid courage, not only wrote a long and brilliant epic, *The Far Horizon,* in which he assessed the horror of the Stalin years. He was transforming his magazine, *Novy Mir,* into a citadel for new talent. Here a dissenting critic was given a platform. Here an experimental novelist could publish. Here a poet could print poems which aroused the party's ire.

It was Konstantin Paustovsky whose name was on the lips of young and old intellectuals. Paustovsky, at seventy, honored and secure, was devoting himself to forging strong links between Russia's past and Russia's future.

In the autumn of 1961 there was published in the provincial town of Kaluga, northwest of Moscow, a volume called *Leaves from Tarussia.* Tarussia was an old Russian village, a village of log huts where the Russian blouse and the stout Russian *valenki,* or felt boots, still survived. The landscape was simple and unspoiled, a region of meadows and forest glades, of small streams and fallen trees, dirt roads and scythe-cut hay. Before and after the Revolution it was a refuge for Russian painters and poets. Marina Tsvetaeva, Ivan Bunin, Vsevolod Ivanov, Zabolitzky and Meyerhold loved the simple beauty of Tarussia.

In *Leaves from Tarussia* Paustovsky gathered works by and about this older generation. To these he joined material of contemporary writers whom he felt linked in spirit to what he called the Tarussia school. This school he equated with the Barbizon school of France, drawing an analogy between the beauty and peace of the French countryside around Fontainebleau and the peculiarly Russian landscape of Tarussia.

Critics contended that Paustovsky's comparison was inapt. They denied that there had appeared a "Tarussia ethic," an identifiable Tarussian approach to art and literature. The writers grouped by Paustovsky were, the critics asserted, in no way different from the main stream of Russian tradition.

In this, it seemed to me, the critics missed the whole point. The Tarussia school was *the* Russian school, the quintessence of the Russian school and that was its significance.

The young Tarussia writers and those of the other new movements were often called by older critics "The Fourth Generation"—the fourth generation since the Revolution. In that phrase was expressed the distance in time and in out-look which separated them from the mood and emotions of 1917. Forty-five years had passed. The members of the Fourth Generation knew the Revolution only through what they had been told and what they had read. They had come to adult-hood since World War II. Most of them had only childhood remembrances of the terrible purges of the 1930's. Many were too young to have served in the last war. To some even Stalin was only a word in a childish song, sung in school, a portrait on the wall, a statue in the park.

But the Fourth Generation was not what the young men and women called themselves. The term they used was "The Men of the Sixties." This phrase is meaningless in English but redolent of associations in Russian.

Of all the facets of the present-day Soviet intelligentsia I found none which impressed me as deeper in implications, more clearly in the broad stream of Russian liberalism, than this designation, the Men of the Sixties.

What did this phrase mean to Russians?

After the long, cruel reign of Nicholas I finally ended and Alexander II mounted the Russian throne, abolishing serf-dom and clearing the way for an Indian summer of liberalism in the 1860's, there emerged a group of writers, critics, poets and philosophers who were known as "The Men of the Sixties." They brought into Russian life a breath of spirit and change. They were the precursors of the radicals who arose twenty-five or thirty years later and carried Russia on through the downfall of czarism and the birth of a new order which (as they confidently believed) would bring forth a flowering of national freedom such as had long been dreamed.

Thus, by calling themselves the Men of the Sixties, the new writers had set their compass by the oldest and best standards of their country. The implications were hardly to be lost upon party men, who still lived, essentially, by the cramped and narrow doctrines evolved by and for Stalin.

It was against this background that I went one night to Chaikovsky Hall to see a spectacle about which all Moscow was talking. This was a presentation by Nikolai Okhlopov, once an associate of the martyred Meyerhold, of Euripedes' *Medea*. No one knew when, if ever, the play had been shown in Moscow before. I had been surprised at the furor it aroused. Tickets were selling at a premium and were difficult to get at any price.

But once the performance was under way I could feel how it swept up the audience. Chaikovsky Hall was an amphitheater with an open stage which was built at Meyerhold's design. But the great director was arrested and exiled to Siberia, where he died during the war before he ever got to use it. So instead of housing experimental theatrical productions it became a concert hall. Now, for the first time, Okhlopov was employing it as it had been designed to be used. He had a great choir ranged in the galleries at either side of the stage. There was a masked Greek chorus on the stage itself and in the center of the amphitheater he placed a full symphony orchestra with spectators sitting all around and in front.

Complex and unusual as were these techniques, powerful as was the acting of Evgenia Kozyreva as Medea, dramatic as was Okhlopov's direction—none of this accounted for the effect on the audience. I saw men and women leave the theater stunned—as though they had stood at the pit of human tragedy and looked into its depths. The play was presented by Okhlopov as an epic of the human spirit rebelling against insupportable injustice. Medea's revenge was that of a soul driven to destroy itself and its world by the blind cruelty of impossible fate.

The more I pondered the strange, terrible mood created by *Medea,* the more certain I felt that those who watched it were drawn back once more to the faceless terror of the Stalin era when, but for a chance of luck, they might have shared the black agonies of Medea.

And this impression became conviction when I read in the program note Okhlopov's hope that "in the spectacle will be heard the angry and proud voice of the greatest of ancient poets raised in the defense of man, his rights and his dignity."

Across Mayakovsky Square from Chaikovsky Hall there was a modest theater which in the winter of 1961-62 was the most popular in Moscow. For most of its plays tickets were sold out several weeks in advance. And for one called *The Four,* by Konstantin Simonov, it took influence to get seats. This was the Contemporary Theater, started three years previously without a building of its own. The year before, it had acquired these premises. It was the nearest thing Moscow possessed to New York's off-Broadway movement. It was an experimental theater of ideas. At least twice, I was told, it had withdrawn controversial works, dealing with seamy aspects of Communism under Stalin, because the repercussions might have jeopardized the theater's very existence. The withdrawals were not from cowardice but from common sense. And each year the theater had succeeded in becoming a little bolder.

The reason why Simonov's *The Four* was a smash hit was because the Moscow public believed that, in the guise of a study of an American writer, conscience-stricken because he has betrayed his friends to a McCarthyite inquisition, Simonov had written his own *mea culpa.* By a simple bit of mental transposition the audience substituted for the American setting a Moscow environment. The victims became Russian writers and wartime comrades. The inquisition was that of Beria and the soul-searching central figure was that of Simonov himself.

Nearly twenty years ago on my first visit to Central Asia I met in Tashkent a striking young couple. The man was a typical Leningrad intellectual, a composer of ability. His wife was an attractive and talented woman whose father had been long stationed in England with a Soviet purchasing mission. Her English was better than mine.

The young composer had been swept up in one of the periodic waves of arrests which sent thousands of Leningrad youth into exile in the years after the murder of Sergei Kirov. His crime was that he had been friendly in high school with another young man who was charged with being a "Trotskyite." For this crime he had been exiled to Tashkent and his sweetheart—like generations of Russian women before her—had married him so that she could share his life in exile.

The couple lived in the old city of Tashkent, the Uzbek part where the houses were made of baked mud and arranged around interior courtyards in which fruit trees and roses grew, watered by the irrigation streams that flowed through the quarter. They had made a new life for themselves in Uzbekistan, studying its history and culture, and out of this had been born the first Uzbek opera, the music written by Alexei Kozlovsky and the score by his wife.

I saw the opera, dealing with the life of Tamerlane's grandson, Ulug Bek, presented at the Tashkent Opera House. The Uzbek authorities were proud of this first flowering of "Uzbek" culture and the composer and his wife hoped that perhaps they might eventually be permitted to return to their beloved Leningrad and rejoin the main stream of Russian intellectual existence.

These memories flooded back to me one day in 1962 when I took down from the shelf of the principal music store in Moscow the lavishly printed, bound and illustrated score of the opera, *Ulug Bek,* just published by the State Musical Publishing House.

How long it had taken the Kozlovskys to get back to Leningrad I did not know. But there was no doubt in my mind that this handsome volume was in part a way of making good on a long-standing, unjust debt owed to two young people of genius.

A few days later there occurred the event of the Moscow musical season, the first performance by the Moscow Philharmonic Orchestra of Shostakovich's Fourth Symphony. Shostakovich wrote the Fourth more than twenty-five years ago. In April of 1936 it was under rehearsal by the Leningrad Symphony Orchestra for its premiere. But that premiere never took place. Just before the concert Shostakovich suddenly withdrew the work, pleading that he had "creative doubts" as to its worth. It was no secret in musical circles as to the source of those "creative doubts." At this time he had been struck by the first of the devastating critical assaults

[41]

by party music censors which were to turn his career into a nightmare. His famous opera, *Lady Macbeth from Mtsensk,* had been denounced so savagely that it vanished from the repertoire for more than twenty-five years. Indeed, his whole future was for a time in jeopardy.

Now at long last the wrong done to Shostakovich, too, was being righted and his symphony (which contemporary Soviet critics found marked by movements of great force and vividness, as well as some imperfections) was taken from the vault where it had long gathered dust and presented to the public.

It was quite clear to me that the movement of the new "Men of the Sixties" was by no means confined simply to the writing field. Hardly a day passed but I heard of new stirrings in other intellectual and artistic activities. The painters, perhaps more bedeviled than any other segment of the intelligentsia, were sticking to their guns. The young men were moving toward abstract impressionism and the new concepts developed in the West. Perhaps they still had to earn their living preparing show window displays or exhibitions for trade fairs (where great artistic license was permitted), but in the private painting which they exhibited in their studios they were doing their best to rejoin the main stream of world art. Not a few found that even though abstract impressionism was still banned in All-Union Art exhibitions it was welcomed in textile and wallpaper design.

Wherever I looked I found ferment among thinking, talented Russians. Was there some central theme to this ferment? Was there a credo broad enough to encompass the Tarussia school, the new mood in music, the often confused strivings of the young painters and sculptors?

There was, or so I strongly believed. The central question of the intellectuals and the artists was: What is truth? And, particularly, what is truth in Russia?

[42]

As had generation after generation before them, the new Men of the Sixties were asking questions—questions to which often neither they nor anyone else had the answer, questions that cut right to the bone of Soviet society and the whole course of Russian life for the past forty years.

They were asking these questions tentatively when I was in Russia in 1959. But now, with the impetus of the Twenty-second Party Congress and its new and sweeping revelations of the scope of Stalin's crimes and the hypocrisy of the whole Stalin era, the questions were being put with an eloquence and a fervor which matched those raised by the original Men of the Sixties in the nineteenth century.

One evening at Moscow University several older writers appeared before a group of students to discuss the task of creative literature. The only question which the young people wanted to talk about was truth—truth and its relationship to the writer. Only the truth, they felt, was worth writing. But where was truth to be found in Soviet society?

No better statement of the credo of the Men of the Sixties had been made, I felt, than that of the new author Mikhail Zlatagorov, who said:

"There is nothing in the world more important than truth. You cannot solve a single problem in life unless you say to yourself: This is good and this is bad. For this I am ready to give up my life. And this I hate and despise. What is truth? Purity of heart."

The sincerity of this statement stemmed from the idealistic extremism which inspired Russian society during the nineteenth century. It had nothing in common with the cant of Soviet "idealism."

What sort of principles did these people stand for? Their creed was related to the finest in Western liberal thought. But there was an important difference. They stood for the

maintenance of the Soviet system and the Communist basis
of the regime, for state ownership of the means of production,
for the social organization of society and for the continuance
of the Soviet state. But they believed in the rule of law and
of justice as it was known in the West, in the freedom of the
individual within socially recognized bounds, in freedom for
the creative arts and in opportunity for the artist to develop
along the lines of his individual personality, and in close
and meaningful state and personal relations between the
Soviet Union and the West. They felt themselves part of
Russia and they felt that Russia was part of the West and, in
turn, of the world.

I was not surprised to find that three events of the past
few months had shocked them. The first was the resumption
of nuclear testing by the Soviet government. The second
was the armed invasion of Goa by India. And the third was
the legal offensive taken against the American Communist
party by the U. S. government.

Each action violated, in a different sense, the principles
which the Men of the Sixties ascribed to the three countries.
They had believed their government was sincere in its pledge
never to test again. They had believed Nehru's doctrine of
nonviolence was universal and that India would abide by it.
And they had believed American democracy would uphold
the freedom of even the most objectionable minority.

Naturally, the Men of the Sixties did not go unchallenged.
Their views were under constant attack by men who, essentially, represented the continuance of the old Stalin policies
of repression in new guises.

No one had brought down more critical lightning than
the young poet Yevgeny Yevtushenko, whose bravado had captured the whole Fourth Generation much as his prototype,

Vladimir Mayakovsky, captured the imagination of the Revolutionary youth.

His public appearances touched off riots and demonstrations. Not infrequently the police had to be called to maintain order when it was announced that he would give a reading of his poems.

None of his colleagues better expressed the contempt felt for their critics than Yevtushenko, who wrote:

> They tell me: Man, you're bold!
> But that is not true. Courage was never my strong point.
> I simply considered it beneath my dignity
> To fall to the level of my colleagues' cowardice. . . .
> One day posterity will remember . . .
> This strange era, these strange times, when
> Ordinary common honesty was called courage.

These men faced the future with confidence. They were aware of the dangers which filled the world; of the trials that lay ahead in their own land; of the distance which had to be traveled before the victory for truth and justice might be won. But the young had the courage of their years and, as the older men said: "We are too old to be afraid."

They numbered in their ranks the flower of Russia's intellect. It was an inspiration to talk with them, to watch the brightness of their eyes, the enthusiasm in their voices.

On a white and snowy Sunday in January I boarded a suburban electric train and rode out to Peredelkino. It was January 7, Russian Orthodox Christmas, and it seemed an appropriate moment for a pilgrimage to the grave of Boris Pasternak. I had last been in the beautiful old village on a sunny Easter Sunday in 1959 and I could still feel the clasp of Pasternak's strong hand on my own and hear his deep and melodious voice in my ear as I stood talking with him for a few moments in the yard of his weather-stained *dacha*.

I plodded through snowdrifts to the summit of the little hill where the poet was buried just a stone's throw from the blue, rose and white village Church of the Transfiguration. The snow around the plain black marble slab which still rested against a pine stake to mark his grave had been heavily trampled by pilgrims. There was a fresh wreath of pine and a winter-frosted bouquet of white chrysanthemums. I laid a spray of cedar on the stone and looked about me.

Across the snowy field was Pasternak's dacha, with that of his friend Konstantin Fedin beside it. Suddenly I realized I was looking at the scene which was in Pasternak's eyes as he wrote the lines to a Christmas star in *Doctor Zhivago*:

> It was winter
> The wind blew from the steppe
> And it was cold for the child
> In the cave of the hillside. . . .
> Far away were a snowy field, a graveyard,
> Fences, tombstones
> The shaft of a cart in a snowdrift
> And above the graveyard a skyful of stars.

Two youngsters on skis made their way up the brow of the hill. "*Posmotri, Vanya*," one of them called. "Watch me!"

Behind me the bells of the little chapel began to toll in the strident, repetitive cadence of the Russian peal. Out from the chapel streamed black-coated peasant women, men and women of the working class and here and there members of the intelligentsia in gray karakul collars and hats. The crowd scattered through the streets and now and then one made his way to Pasternak's grave, pausing there a moment and then moving on.

How good it would be, I pondered, if Pasternak had lived on to see the Fourth Generation grow in strength, to listen to the new Men of the Sixties as they fought the battles of truth. And yet, I thought as I made my way under the snow-bowed pines back toward the suburban railroad station, that was not really necessary. The torch which Pushkin held was grasped from his dying hand by Lermontov. And Belinsky carried it later. Then there were Chernyshevsky, Dobrolyubov, Tolstoy, Turgenev, Chekhov—all the rest. There had always been a hand ready to carry it on, no matter how difficult the time. And this, of course, Pasternak had well known, long before he went to his homely resting place on the little hill beside the meadow of Peredelkino.

4. The Growth of Neo-Stalinism

THE WINDOW of my room at the National Hotel looked out on Manezhny Square and, beyond the square, to the soft, rose-colored walls of the Kremlin. I could look past the Historical Museum right into Red Square itself and see the Mausoleum, the great Spassky Clock Tower and St. Basil's Cathedral.

On the morning of December 21, 1961, the line of visitors waiting to see the Mausoleum extended back through the square, snaking down beside the Historical Museum and through the iron gates of the Alexander Gardens almost as far as I could see. It was not a particularly long line. The Mausoleum was open five days a week and I had seen from my window some lines that were longer, some that were shorter. Just after eleven o'clock the line began to move through the tomb and I went down from the hotel and joined it. My interest was stirred by the fact that this was the eighty-second anniversary of the birth of Josef Stalin and

I wondered whether there would be any special reaction to this among the visitors. I quickly found that there was not. Few people realized that it was Stalin's anniversary. Most were from out of town. They were more interested in seeing what had been done with Stalin's body—removed from the Mausoleum only a few weeks previously—than in viewing that of Lenin, which remained. When the line, moving rapidly, reached the Mausoleum I noticed that the basalt blocks which carried the inscription "Lenin/Stalin" over the entrance had not been removed but only masked with a piece of fiberboard, colored to resemble stone, on which the word "Lenin" had been painted in none-too-accurate brush strokes. Within the tomb there was more evidence of haste. Stalin's sarcophagus had been removed but that of Lenin had not been centered. It was still to one side just where it had been moved in 1953 to permit the placing of Stalin's body.

As soon as we were out in daylight again the line almost broke into a dog trot past the Red Square reviewing stands and around back of the Mausoleum to the little graveyard where the heroes of Communism are buried, some in urns in the Kremlin wall and some in conventional graves beside it. Stalin's grave was a conventional one, with a simple dark stone of polished granite, bearing his name and the dates of his birth and death in gold lettering. It was the last grave in a row just beside that of Mikhail Kalinin, the former Soviet President. Each of the other graves was marked by a bust as well as a headstone and this fact stimulated considerable controversy among the visitors. Would a bust of Stalin be put up?

"Certainly, comrades," said a man in army uniform. "They have to erect a bust. It's simply required."

"Don't be so sure," a companion, also in uniform, said.

[49]

"Remember only a few weeks ago it said 'Lenin/Stalin' over the Mausoleum. Now it says only 'Lenin.' "

A small man from Rostov stood for a moment or two before the grave. "Well, no flowers on his grave," he sighed.

"That's right," an elderly, mustached visitor responded, "not even a forget-me-not."

As I walked across Red Square, past St. Basil's over to the bustling GUM department store I could not help remembering a story I had heard just a few night before.

Kalinin, Stalin's neighbor beside the Kremlin wall, asks the old Dictator: "How long are you going to be here?"

Stalin replies: "At least until the Twenty-third Party Congress."

Kalinin: "Then where will you go?"

Stalin: "Wherever the party sends me."

Later in the day I telephoned Tbilisi to see how Stalin's birthday had been marked in his native Georgia. The answer was it had not been. I well remembered the rioting which swept Tbilisi in March, 1956, touched off by Khrushchev's famous secret speech denouncing Stalin. Now the denunciations of the Twenty-second Party Congress and the public effacement of Stalin symbols had been accepted with some complaisance. In part this was because the Georgians were becoming habituated to Stalin's new status. In part it was due to greater sophistication. The 1962 denigration was not carried so far in the Georgian press and for many months his statues were not disturbed. The shrine at his birthplace in the mountain village of Gori remained open, although visitors were few. The great hotel, just completed at the time of Stalin's death, often had only a handful of guests.

I found no great rush in the provinces to obliterate the name and fame of Stalin. True, the hundred-foot statue on which Stalin had lavished thirty-three tons of pure copper had been taken down from the entrance to the Volga-Don canal. The big figure of Stalin in the heroic central square of Stalingrad had been removed (between 3 A.M. and 6 A.M. one night) and the citizens of the hero city of World War II were gradually learning to say "Volgograd" after a week in which all the signs had been taken down and they did not know what their city's name would be.

But in Siberia, the Ukraine and Central Asia hundreds of Stalin statues still stood in public parks. Fly-specked piles of Stalin portraits lay on the counters of bookstores and an occasional Stalin picture was to be seen in an office or public waiting room. It would be a long, long time before the mark of Stalin was erased from Russia's sprawling body.

In Moscow the task of reducing Stalin to something less than life size proceeded apace. It was not long before a wooden fence went up around the Mausoleum. Stonemasons put back the old "Lenin" pediment which had been there before Stalin was moved into the tomb and Lenin's coffin was once again put in the center of the chamber. Teams of workmen descended into the Moscow subway system. They chiseled out Stalin's name wherever it appeared. His face was painted over in the murals and where it could not be obliterated from the mosaics new ones were glued up.

One day I went to the Lenin Museum. Once Stalin had been as prominent here as Lenin. I found only five pictures of the old Generalissimo, mostly small photographs showing him as a young revolutionary. In contrast there was a big layout of materials about Khrushchev—oil paintings, collections of his works and memorabilia.

The most striking disappearance of the Stalin image was provided by the All-Union Art Exhibition in Manezhny Hall. Just twelve years before I had counted the Stalin works in the 1949 exhibit—nearly seventy in a collection of about six hundred paintings. The 1961 exhibition boasted not a single Stalin picture. As I was interested to note, there were eight heroic paintings of Khrushchev showing him with Ukrainian peasants, Baku oil workers and, even, American dock workers in San Francisco. Adulation of Khrushchev was far from equaling the obsequiousness shown Stalin but it was nonetheless notable that no other living Russian political figure was depicted in the 1961 exhibition.

By and large Stalin's name was being erased with a ruthlessness and totality which were both Russian and Soviet.

The public had accepted this with passivity colored with some surprise. They had not expected the new bolts of lightning. It was different with the intellectuals, officials, publicists, the movers and doers of Soviet society. For them, the key fact was not the symbolic removal of Stalin from the Mausoleum. For them the key was Stalinism, the body of thought, of doctrine, of political habits and theory, of style and atmosphere indelibly associated with Stalin's name.

What about Stalinism? Was it being wiped out with the same meticulousness as the icons of Stalin? The answer was by no means clear. The speeches at the Twenty-second Party Congress had set off a whole new wave of de-Stalinization. History was being tidied up. In the military field this was noticeable. Commanders like Tukhachevsky and Blücher had been restored to their rightful places. The charges of treason had been lifted. No longer was Stalin portrayed as the hero of the Battle of Tsaritsyn. His errors in the 1920 war with Poland were being exposed. So were those he committed in 1939 and 1941.

The victims of the purges had been more fully rehabilitated. This was particularly true for the purges of 1937 and the years following. History continued to be distorted so far as Trotsky, Zinoviev, Kamenev and Bukharin were concerned but even they no longer were "un-persons." Their names reappeared and some of the heat and vindictiveness had vanished.

The flaws in the Stalin record were being picked over—as far back as the days of the 1905 Russian Revolution. He was exposed for what he was—a minor Caucasian revolutionary who sometimes could be found on one side and again on the other side of questions which agitated the underground Marxist movement. It was now recalled (as Trotsky often had noted in his lifetime) that Stalin was a bad Leninist as well as a bad Marxist. Error without end was exposed in Stalin's economics, his theories of government, his attempts at doctrine, his interference in the fields of law, literature and science.

His victims were beginning to lose their reticence about speaking in public of their suffering at Stalin's hands. Two years previously I had met Russian acquaintances who had come back from terms in Stalin's Siberian prison camps. I knew they had come back and they knew that I knew. But nothing was said on either side. The topic was just beginning to be discussed in novels and plays. This shyness had vanished. One night a celebration was held in honor of Sergei Obratzov, the wonderful creator of puppets. It was Obratzov's sixtieth birthday and most of Moscow's literati turned out. The master of ceremonies was Vladimir Alexeiev, who told of spending "some years away from Moscow in a certain place."

"There," he said, "we had all the most talented people— the best writers, the best actors, the best directors, the best artists. It was the best collective in the country. We were all in different grades—the two-year class, the four-year class and the ten-year class. But not higher than the ten-year class."

Out in Siberia, he said, they had organized their own cultural and artistic life and one of the activities was a puppet

[53]

show patterned after Obratzov's. The highest tribute to their efforts came when the guards at the morning roll call started calling the prisoners not by their family names but by those of the roles they played in the puppet shows.

At a Kremlin meeting a similar matter-of-fact tone was set by Galina Serebryakova, a veteran Communist party figure who had just published a fictionalized biography of Marx and Engels. In a talk about Communist propaganda Mme. Serebryakova recalled that "I myself spent twenty years in prison," sometimes under torture and solitary confinement. Her experience was not unlike that related to the Twenty-second Party Congress by another old Bolshevik, Alexandra Lazurkina, who told how she had been arrested as a member of the Leningrad party apparatus in 1937. She spent seventeen years in the prison camps, all the time faithful to her belief in Stalin. She was certain he did not know of her fate.

So they talked quite openly. Perhaps this was the beginning of a new expression of liberal viewpoints in Russia. But there was another face to the coin. This was the crystallization of neo-Stalinism—a political tendency which paid lip service to de-Stalinization but which advocated and employed the old Stalinist techniques in only slightly disguised form.

Leonid F. Ilyichev, Premier Khrushchev's chief propagandist, had created the ideological umbrella under which the neo-Stalinists were moving forward. This was what Moscow had nicknamed the "cult of authority" or the "cult of leadership" as opposed to the Stalin cult, which was ordinarily referred to in the dialectic jargon as the "cult of personality."

Ilyichev advanced his convenient concept at the Twenty-second Party Congress, in which he warned that it would be "incorrect and harmful to confuse the prestige of leaders and the cult of personality." The idea was that the party must maintain the prestige of its leaders while at the same time dismantling the Stalinist "cult of personality."

If this sounded like an attempt to carry water on both shoulders it was not surprising. Ilyichev had been practicing that feat for many years. He served as one of Stalin's chief propagandists, first as editor of the newspaper *Izvestia* and later as editor of *Pravda*. Now that Stalin was in bad odor Ilyichev found it convenient to stress the difficulties he had encountered working for Stalin—the reproofs and reprimands which had come his way. With his chief, the austere Mikhail A. Suslov, Ilyichev was one of the few men who had made the transition from Stalin to Khrushchev without missing a single pulse beat.

Now Ilyichev was rapidly becoming a power in his own right. A man with a talent for practical press arrangements, a quick and sarcastic wit, a ruthless and driving ambition, he had demonstrated his value to Khrushchev as the head of a quasi-official "Press Group" which Khrushchev set up to handle Kremlin public relations, particularly in connection with his frequent trips to the West. The Twenty-second Party Congress placed Ilyichev within the party Secretariat, but whether as ally, rival or henchman of Suslov, perhaps neither of them would quite know until the showdown came.

Nor could one quite be certain that Ilyichev's neo-Stalinist line emanated (as many in Moscow thought) from Suslov. Suslov was the one man within Khrushchev's leadership group who had almost no contact with foreigners—except foreign Communists. He remained an enigma, although some comrades from the West who had to deal with him said he had the coldest, cruelest personality of any man in the Kremlin. In fairness it could be added that there were others who insisted that Suslov was a warm, gentle, intelligent man with a quiet, retiring personality. But there were few in Moscow who did not believe that Suslov felt more comfortable within the framework of Stalinism than within that of Khrushchevism.

Nor was Suslov alone in this. It was becoming harder and harder for old-line party bosses—the regional secretaries, the factory managers, the construction chiefs, the state farm executives—to get the results which Khrushchev demanded without the lash of police fear, authoritarianism, compulsion, arrests and punishment which they had been able to wield under Stalin. Their jobs and their futures were at stake in this. And the party wheel horses were not alone. There was a hard driving, younger party group impatient for action, impatient for position, careless of methods, intolerent of opposition. They were eager to get on with the job and didn't mind much how it was done.

The hallmark of the neo-Stalinist line was rough, tough, bullyboy tactics (or language) invariably invoked in the name of some supposed state or social aim.

For example, a group of young Moscow architects set up a small café just off Sadovo-Karetny Ryad in an old run-down building. The neighborhood had been poor since long before the Revolution but the location was central. They named the café Aelita after the heroine of a novel of that name, a girl from Mars. The novel was written by Alexei Tolstoy during his period of emigration. It was published in Russia but was not liked by Stalin and long since had gone out of print.

The architects' café was designed as a pleasant place where young people could gather in the evening to read poetry, discuss artistic questions and spend a few hours in intellectually stimulating conversation. Neither vodka nor beer was sold. Admission—at least at the start—was by invitation.

Soon, however, a gang of Young Communist bullies appeared.

"We hear that foreigners are interested in this place," said a hard-nosed young man. "There must be something wrong with it."

A sentry was stationed at the door and the pleasant, relaxed atmosphere of this timid experiment was quickly destroyed. These bullies were the same as those who formed the original core of the druzhina, the voluntary police auxiliary. They were the same who in 1961 assaulted girls who appeared in pedal pushers and toreador trousers on the beaches at Sochi, insisting that they be arrested for "indecency." They were the same who tried forcibly to compel young men to shave off their "Castro" beards and who ripped their pencil-thin trousers.

Their chief organ was the Young Communist newspaper, *Komsomolskaya Pravda,* and in its columns there appeared repeated attempts to link and to confuse liberal and nonconformist tendencies with really decadent forces, such as currency speculation, "parasitism," idling, hooliganism, moonshining, black marketing, embezzlement and, even, security violations. In this and other organs, it was often difficult to find any line of distinction between a surrealist painter and a pimp, between a writer of realistic short stories and the youthful delinquents whom he was describing.

The strength of the group was to be found in the same curious coalition of the Communist Youth movement, the security police, reactionary literary circles, Stalinist ideologists and party hacks which formed the center of an attempt in autumn, 1958, to stampede Khrushchev back to a Stalinist course.

The 1958 campaign reached its climax in a disgusting per-

sonal assault upon Boris Pasternak carried out in the presence
of Khrushchev by a man named Vladimir V. Semichastny,
then head of the Communist Youth organization. There were
a number of sinister facets to the campaign but none more
sinister than a deliberate attempt to arouse the Russian working class against the Russian intelligentsia by charging that
the intelligentsia had been disloyal and unreliable at the time
of the Hungarian and Polish crises in 1956. The key figure
in the smear campaign was the ambitious propagandist Vsevolod Kochetov, who customarily presented his ideas in the
form of badly constructed, pedestrianly written novels.

The cabal overreached itself in 1958. Khrushchev apparently sensed their true objectives and all of the leading
participants were reprimanded, demoted or chastised in some
way. But not permanently.

I found them all back on the scene, bigger than ever and
more powerful than ever, in 1961. Semichastny had returned
from obscurity in Turkmenistan to take over the chairman-
ship of the Committee on State Security from his close friend
and associate, Alexander N. Shelepin (himself a former
Young Communist chief). Sergei P. Pavlov, the new head of
the Young Communists, was making speeches similar to those
of Semichastny in earlier years. And Kochetov had just
finished a new novel, called *Secretary of the Regional Committee,* which was even more openly aggressive and reactionary than his 1958 production, *The Brothers Yershov.*
The new novel called for death penalties against all kinds
of social offenders. It was permeated with hostility toward
the Soviet intelligentsia. It caricatured leading liberal figures
as libertines, fools and scoundrels. It called for an end of
private ownership of country cottages and automobiles and
attacked in scurrilous terms persons who built their own
homes and maintained their own fruit and vegetable gardens.

Personal cars, Kochetov contended, should be reserved for government and party chiefs. Country houses should be provided only to those whom the state deemed deserving.

The hero of Kochetov's novel was, by his own description, a leader of the "new type," drawn, somewhat, to resemble Khrushchev. The villain was a leader of the "old type," a kind of provincial Stalin who ruled by dictate and liked to telephone his subordinates at 3 A.M., as Stalin did.

While envy and jealousy and a drive for power seemed clearly to be among the motivations behind the neo-Stalinist platform, there was no doubt that it commanded widespread support within the party. So strong were the rumors before the Twenty-second Party Congress that ownership of dachas and automobiles would be forbidden that many persons sold their homes and cars at sacrifice prices. When Krushchev was told of the rumors he said it was nonsense. Prices went back to normal.

But the insistence upon punitive hostility toward specific kinds of social offenders was not nonsense. It represented the dominant line of Soviet policy and it was already seriously burdening the new and little-tested foundations of the Soviet rule of law which—not without difficulty—had been introduced since Stalin's death.

The neo-Stalinists were advocating and practicing mob rule and lynch law. They called on courts to take punitive action against offenders. They organized and praised mobs which entered the courtrooms and hissed and abused defendants, putting on more and more pressure for extreme sentences. The targets were known criminals, speculators, currency offenders, former Nazi collaborators, persons who had no claim on public sympathy. But the invocation of ex post facto law for these offenders boded ill for the tenuously established fabric of a rule of justice.

So often the same men—and Kochetov was a notable example—who praised death sentences for social offenders deliberately blurred the line between drunkenness and speculation and an interest in Western art and culture or a taste for innovation in music or painting.

Young men who sought to paint in the style of abstract impressionism and writers who realistically portrayed nihilistic youth were assaulted as though they were seeking to undermine the foundations of Soviet society.

Behind the façade of Soviet society there were telltale marks of linkage between the old secret police and the new, between the police, the Communist Youth, the druzhina, the "comradely courts" set up to police factory workers and the "neighborly courts" set up to police apartment house dwellers. The combination of secret police and Komsomol associates which joined forces against currency speculators was found using the same mechanisms to entrap foreigners and attempt to enlist them in their espionage network.

One did not need to know Russia well to perceive that a dangerous coalition of forces existed, one which might well turn the clock back again to some point close to where it stood at the hour of Stalin's death.

But this would not necessarily prove an easy task. In the Stalin years any voice of protest was automatically choked off. Siberia or the firing squad was the fate of those who challenged the Stalin way. Today the neo-Stalinists were confronted with formidable opponents. The main weight of the Soviet intelligentsia was backing the liberalizing tendency. There was no sign that the attacks of the neo-Stalinists had intimidated them. To the contrary. They controlled powerful organs with which to present their views. The journal *Novy Mir* watched the rise of neo-Stalinism with hawklike intensity. The magazine *Yunost (Youth)* stuck to its

[60]

guns until the Stalinist writer Boris Polevoi was installed as its editor, and even then the courageous young *Yunost* writers declined to be silenced. The literary newspaper *Literaturnaya Gazetta* was found on the liberal side most of the time and the liberal tendency spoke not infrequently from the pages of *Pravda* and *Izvestia.*

This was by no means accidental. As *Novy Mir* pointed out in an extremely sharp counterattack on the neo-Stalinists in January, 1962, there was reason to believe that some, at least, of them had secretly opposed Khrushchev in his struggle with the antiparty group of Molotov, Malenkov and Kaganovich in June, 1957. Moreover, *Novy Mir* charged, the neo-Stalinists were seeking to form a factional clique or intraparty power grouping—a most serious violation of Communist party regulations.

Novy Mir buttressed its attack with a devastating analysis of Kochetov's new novel, demonstrating that Kochetov's "leader of a new type" was a man who was unable to accept the revelation of Stalin's crimes and who himself ruled just as much by dictate as his outwardly Stalinist antagonist. He was, in fact, the prototype of the neo-Stalinist.

Tvardovsky, the plain-spoken editor of *Novy Mir,* underlined the position of the intellectuals in a public address in which he bluntly declared that the time had passed when any one organ could lay down a literary line in Russia. He said that the days of the "dogmatists" had ended.

Thus, for the first time within my knowledge of the Soviet Union, an open struggle was going forward between two powerful groups, one neo-Stalinist and the other "liberal," for the dominant role in the country's future. I needed no guide to tell me that the outcome would profoundly affect Moscow's relations with the West and the whole nature of her internal evolution. It was equally clear that the struggle could not go forward unless there was strong support at the top for each tendency. What was in progress was a war of words between advocates of contending viewpoints, struggling for the minds of the Soviet people. It was being waged under the curious limitations of Soviet dictatorship.

It was not possible to evaluate accurately the comparative weight of these forces nor to predict which might win. But the fact that the struggle could go on was evidence of the evolution of Soviet society and the distance it had traveled from the rigidity of Stalin's day. The Twenty-second Party Congress had given this tendency breadth and momentum. But neo-Stalinism had emerged as a great danger, operating through quasi-legal or extra-legal ruffianism reminiscent of Nazi methods.

5. The Rise of Anti-Semitism

THE EVENING was raw and dark and the car picked its way through the ill-lighted streets with difficulty. We had come down the high bluff, passed through the old commercial area of Kiev and plunged into the Podol, the traditional Jewish quarter, where the stores were poor and crowded, the houses down-at-the-heels and the courtyards cluttered with debris. The driver missed his turn but finally pulled up in front of a dark brick building. The entrance was barred by an iron grille but a gate at one side led to the rear. This was the Kiev synagogue and it looked closed but as soon as I pushed through the gate a venerable bearded figure stepped out of the shadows and spoke: "*Otkuda vye?* Where are you from?" It was the traditional challenge, a bit like "Who goes there?" I had heard it often enough from policemen and guards and it put me off. "*Iz Amerika.* From America," I replied. "I've come to visit the synagogue."

Our shoes clattered on the broken pavement as we made

our way to a side door and entered a long, low-ceilinged room where half a dozen men were gathered around a plain deal table on which was heaped a pile of bills, receipts and miscellaneous business papers. Two men, both burly, wide-shouldered and Russian-appearing, immediately detached themselves and came forward. They, their manner clearly suggested, would do the talking. Their associates shrank back except for the bearded man who stood beside me. I felt immediately that the burly pair were agents of the police, representatives placed in the synagogue to see that things were run in the fashion the authorities wanted them run. Every word they spoke confirmed this belief.

I had come to visit the Kiev synagogue because I had heard so many reports of repressions against the Jewish faith and of rising anti-Semitism. I was sure that if substance lay behind the rumors the Ukraine was the place to find it. For generations the Ukraine had been a seedbed of anti-Semitism. It needed but a hint from Moscow to set it off again.

I said to the broad-shouldered men that I had been told that a number of synagogues had been closed. They knitted their brows. Indeed, they had heard nothing. Of course, if there were not enough people to support one synagogue or another it might be closed. That, I said, was not what I had in mind—had the authorities been closing synagogues? They displayed indignation. What did I mean by a remark like that? Here they had complete freedom to worship and complete freedom not to worship. Just, they added, as you have in America. No difference at all. Obviously, my conversation was going to be devoid of positive content but I wanted to see to what lengths they might carry their sophisms. What was the size of their congregation? They had no statistics. There was no registration of members. How many Jews were there in Kiev? Ask the City Soviet. They themselves had no idea. How many worshipers did they have? About six thousand at the time of the High Holidays. The crowds filled the synagogue and the street outside. Was this the only synagogue in Kiev? Oh, no. There were others.

The old bearded man had listened to the colloquy with mounting emotion, repeatedly muttering to himself. Now he could no longer contain his feelings. "No, that's not true," he burst out. "This is the only one."

The burly men were not nonplused. "We have two more synagogues right here," they said." One upstairs and one in the building just behind. Just wait. We'll get the keys and show you. The one upstairs is very beautiful." There was a little more talk, some jokes about the age of the congregation. Most young people, they said, were not interested in religion. But they had complete freedom to worship if they desired. And the congregation had everything that was needed—their own books, articles of prayer, even a Jewish journal. Often, they had visitors from America. There were many reports spread in America saying that the Jews were badly treated. There was no truth to those reports. I could see this for myself. I smiled sadly and made my way out into the courtyard. The old man with a beard shook his head in despondency. The keys to the "beautiful" synagogues unfortunately could not be found. Perhaps, I would come again. I thanked them and said, *"Sholem aleichem."* Then I got into my taxi and rode back to the Intourist Hotel, along the wide boulevard of the Kreshchatik, the Street of the Cross, so badly damaged by the Nazi occupiers, now fully restored, chestnut trees and all.

Few Russian cities suffered more at the hands of the Germans than Kiev. The number of those executed ran to several hundred thousand. Kiev was not indifferent to the lives sacrificed during the war. High on the cliffs overlooking the Dnieper I visited a monument to all those who died in wartime Kiev. An eternal flame burned there in memory of the victims and each day guides took pilgrims to the spot.

There was no mention at the monument that any Jewish lives had been lost in Kiev. Yet Kiev was the site of one of the most barbaric slaughters of Jews carried out by the Nazi brigades. How many Jews were killed is not known even today. The estimates run between 75,000 and 130,000. Wave after wave of Jews was marched outside the city to an isolated spot. There they were lined up and shot. Each new group was forced to spread earth over the earlier victims. Then they too were mowed down with machine-gun fire. The name of that isolated gully was Babi Yar, and the infamy perpetrated there was known around the world. But when I asked to go there I met a blank wall. "You have to have special permission. There is nothing to see there. It is too difficult." Those were the words of the hotel people. Actually, there was "nothing to see." The place was a desolate ravine. Part was used as a city dump. The municipal council had plans for filling it in and erecting a sports center.

Babi Yar was not a name that Soviet officials liked to hear. When it was mentioned they quickly replied that Jews were not the only people killed by the Nazis. There were Ukrainian and Russian victims, too.

There were many aspects of the Jewish situation which officials did not like to discuss. And there was good reason for this. Once again the Jews were experiencing a time of trouble. It was not so bad as some of the times of the past. There were no pogroms. The old czarist slogan of "Beat the Jews and save Russia" might be muttered by some hooligans but it got no official encouragement. Nor were Jews being arrested on paranoiac charges and shipped off to Siberia. They were not being executed by the secret police.

Nonetheless, the symptoms of fear and suspicion visible at the Kiev synagogue could be found in most Jewish communities. Open anti-Semitism had shown its ugly face in the rural areas of the Ukraine, in parts of Byelorussia and the Moldavian Republic.

Its revival had been stimulated by aggressive official propaganda against the Jewish religion and Zionism, often couched in terms that blurred the boundary between anti-religion and anti-Semitism.

Once again Jews were reluctant to have contact with foreigners because of reprisals which might be visited upon them. The same Young Komsomol gangs which had been thrown into action against the younger generation, against hooligans, against nonconformist liberals, had been mobilized to intimidate Jewish communities. The same xenophobia which marked the reaction of the neo-Stalinists against foreign clothing, foreign styles or foreign tastes was displayed against the Jews.

This was intensified by the phobia which the Communist party always displayed toward any non-Communist social group, regardless of basis. The Jews were a particularly cohesive group and this made them suspect. The Jews had connections with coreligionists abroad and had demonstrated their sympathy for Israel. To the Soviet secret police an interest in Israel was equated with "security risk." Israeli representatives were considered spies and agents of the U.S. Central Intelligence Agency.

The regime made no secret of its suspicions. Two Israeli diplomats were expelled in 1961, one of them Yakov Sharett, son of the former foreign minister. They were charged with spying, spreading of Israeli propaganda and links with the C.I.A. The same charges were publicly made against another

Israeli diplomat, Joshua Pratt. It was claimed that Israeli diplomats used Jewish synagogues to meet with their agents, collect information and spread slander.

Nor was this left a matter solely of newspaper publicity. In October, 1961, G. R. Pechorsky, head of the Jewish community in Leningrad, a notably outspoken man, and two other leading members were tried in semisecrecy and sentenced to long prison terms on charges of "contact with a foreign power," Israel. A similar trial was conducted in Moscow. Word quickly spread through the Jewish communities. The reaction was exactly what might have been anticipated. A few weeks later when a member of the Jewish community in Moscow was asked what he knew of the Pechorsky matter he replied, "We do not know anything about Pechorsky and we do not want to know anything about Pechorsky."

But the matter did not halt there. It was followed by moves against the leaders of most of the important Jewish communities in the Soviet Union. In cities like Riga, Kiev, Vilna, Tashkent and many others the known and respected Jewish leaders were compelled to resign and more complaisant men were put in their place. An effort was initiated to create a public image of Jewish graft, corruption and drunkenness. Propaganda stories were published exposing financial scandals in synagogues. Rabbis were described as drunkards and embezzlers of church funds.

Typical of this was a scurrilous pamphlet issued in Kishinev for local use. It contained "revelations" about drinking and speculation by church elders. A ninety-year-old Jew was made to write of his gratification at having finally learned the "truth" about his corrupt faith. The poor old man was compelled to go about the city, delivering speeches against his church. The same work sought to link the Jews to the

Rumanian occupation forces in Moldavia during World War II and even hinted that the Jews had supported Czar Nicholas II.

In Kishinev and other areas pressure was brought upon members of the Jewish communities to petition the authorities for permission to close synagogues on grounds they were no longer interested in maintaining them. How many synagogues were forced to close through such intimidation was not known but in the Ukraine and Moldavia whole rural regions were left without Jewish places of worship.

A drive was launched against corruption which quickly began to display a deliberate emphasis upon Jewish participants. One case involved a group of speculators arrested in Leningrad in January, 1961, on charges of shipping whole railroad cars filled with private merchandise around the Soviet Union. The chief culprits were identified as Jews. One of them, named Kraizman, was sentenced to death. Another spectacular case was publicized in Tbilisi in which the ringleader was alleged to have been one Mordecai Kakiashvili, the ninety-four-year-old leader of the Jewish community. He was sentenced to death and executed.

Propaganda frequently coupled charges of speculation with nationalist deviation and religious survivals. The Jew was identified in the public mind as a criminal, a grafter, a drunkard, a superstitious religionist and, not infrequently, a traitor.

The security risk charges stemmed from Soviet hypersensitivity to Zionism. Relations had long been bad with Israel and were not improved by Soviet efforts to make political friends among the Arab states. With three million Jews in the Soviet Union the regime suffered qualms about their sympathies with Jews abroad.

Contacts between Jews and Israeli diplomats had tended

to broaden with the general liberalization of the regime. In many cities Jews demonstratively welcomed visits by Israel diplomats. In Leningrad, for example, during the celebration of Simhath Torah in 1959 some 4,000 Jews turned out and serenaded an Israeli diplomat. The next year 7,000 Jews appeared. In October, 1961, the number was between 8,000 and 12,000. The trial of leaders of the Leningrad and Moscow Jewish communities quickly followed the Simhath Torah celebration of October, 1961. This was not a coincidence— or so the Jews felt.

The vigor of Israeli diplomatic activity in Russia and the close contacts of Israelis with Jewish communities were believed by many diplomats to have stimulated the Soviet authorities in carrying out reprisals against Jews. The most prominent victims were persons who had contacts with the diplomats.

There was no evidence that the Israeli activities were anything but legal. None of them would have caused a reaction in any country but Russia. But the Israeli actions roused Soviet security agencies—and the propaganda organs closely allied to them—to a fury of charges.

In part, at least, the Soviet reaction seemed to be contributing to precisely what the authorities feared most—the strengthening of Jewish ties to their coreligionists and to their faith. Many young persons of Jewish origin had almost lost sight of their antecedents. But the virulent anti-Semitism of the late Stalin years coupled with symptoms of resurgence under Khrushchev was making them more and more conscious of their Jewishness.

In the Stalin years I had known Jews who deliberately "lost" their internal passports on which were inscribed the fateful words: "Nationality—Jew." They then applied to the Interior Ministry for new passports, specifying their nationality as Russian. Because many records had been destroyed during the war they often were able to change their nationality successfully and escape the penalties which might have been imposed on them for being Jewish.

Now in the relatively more liberal Khrushchev era young people were insisting on being recorded as Jews. They were telling the census taker that their language was Yiddish although, in fact, they knew only a few words. They were studying German because no classes in Yiddish were offered in the Soviet Union. They were attending the occasional concerts of Yiddish songs and recitations in the Moscow music halls—although they had to have the lyrics and jokes translated. They were buying out each issue of the new Yiddish literary bimonthly, *Sovietish Heimland,* which was appearing in editions of 25,000 to 30,000 copies. They were showing up for services at the synagogues on Friday nights and at holiday times in unusual numbers. They were more conscious of their Jewishness and of the underlying anti-Jewishness (if not anti-Semitism) of the regime than ever before. As one young man of Jewish parentage said: "Three years ago I told my friends that only the last vestiges of anti-Semitism were left in the Soviet Union; that soon it would be entirely gone. I could not have been more wrong. It is stronger here in the Ukraine now than I have ever known it."

And this attitude had its reflection in the older generation. Ilya Ehrenburg, whose anti-Zionist sentiments were well known, a man who for years spoke of himself as a Russian rather than a Jew, a man whose remarks often seemed deliberately weighted with anti-Jewishness, proclaimed over Moscow radio on his seventieth birthday that so long as anti-Semitism persisted he would proudly bear the designation "Jew" on his Soviet passport.

It was in this public rebuke of anti-Semitism that the

Russia of 1962 differed sharply from that of fifteen years earlier. Then, the appearance of anti-Semitism had been marked by silence. The hand of Stalin had been too heavy and the tradition of acceptance of evil persisted long after the old dictator's death.

But now voices challenged the shame. This was in the clear tradition of Russian liberalism. When the Czar permitted the "black hundreds" to ravage the Ukraine with pogroms the intelligentsia spoke up in outrage—Korolenko, Tolstoy, Chekhov, Gorky, each made himself heard against the loathsome outrages. The early years of the Bolshevik regime had been marked by a firm and clear stand against anti-Semitism but under Stalin all this changed and again the Jew became Russia's scapegoat.

Today the great tradition of Russia's past was being carried forward by some of her youngest and most brilliant writers, poets like Yevtushenko and Nekrasov. When they spoke out, the whole of Russia's younger generation—from party-line Young Communists to disillusioned stilyagi—listened and cheered.

There was no single figure on the Soviet literary scene with the mass following of Yevtushenko. A non-Jew, Yevtushenko's poetic denunciations of the continuance and quasi-official encouragement of anti-Semitism were published by the periodical press. He recited his poems to stormy audiences of students in clubs and assemblies all over Moscow. He flaunted his appearances at the Israeli Embassy in Moscow and when he declaimed his poem, "Babi Yar," indicting his fellow citizens for anti-Semitism on Poets' Day in autumn, 1961, in Moscow's Mayakovsky Square the crowd of young people was so great that the police finally intervened.

When the youngsters refused to disperse at midnight,

police vans were summoned. Dozens of youngsters were loaded into the vehicles and driven twenty miles outside town, dumped out and forced to find their way back to the city as best they might. The youngsters demonstrated their support of Yevtushenko and their contempt for the police by reassembling the next night. Once again they refused to disperse and once again were taken out of town and dumped by the roadside.

The neo-Stalinist poet Alexei Markov published a slanderous couplet in one of the principal neo-Stalinist organs, *Literatura i Zhizn,* characterizing Yevtushenko as a "pygmy cosmopolite," lacking in patriotism. A poetic "answer to Markov" promptly began to circulate in hand-written copies among the Moscow intelligentsia. It compared the Stalinist Markov to the notorious anti-Semite of the last czarist days, a man known as "Markov the Second." The Soviet writer was promptly christened "Markov the Third."

The indignation of the intelligentsia did not halt the government in its anti-Jewish program. The harassment went on. At Passover in 1962 Jews in Moscow found it impossible to obtain the traditional matzoth which in the past had always been baked by Moscow bakeries. The publication of Yevtushenko's "Babi Yar" in Yiddish translation was put off from month to month.

Most diplomats in Moscow blamed the regime's insensitivity to the creeping anti-Semitism and the increasing anti-Jewishness to the attitudes of Premier Khrushchev himself. The Soviet leader had often discussed Jewish questions with foreign deputations and invariably displayed not a few of the anti-Semitic prejudices common to the borderland of the Ukraine where he grew up. It was no secret that the Premier liked to tell stories which made a butt of some "poor Yid."

So long as this attitude persisted at the top it seemed unlikely that an objective approach to the problem could be expected in Russia.

Yet, despite all this, "administrative" anti-Semitism, the arbitrary dismissal of Jews from their posts or their sentence to exile or execution, was not occurring. In the Moscow and Leningrad educational systems discrimination against Jewish students was lighter than it had been. The bars to Jewish advancement in diplomatic service, the army or the higher echelons of the party and propaganda apparatus continued. But the key role played by Jewish scientists in space and rocketry had won grudging public recognition.

And, what was most important, the situation was no longer hidden under a veil of terror-stricken silence. The Jews once more had powerful and articulate allies within the Soviet intellectual community who were courageously seeking to arouse Russians to a feeling of shame and anger at the anti-Semitic strain on the national conscience. Change—sooner or later—seemed bound to come.

6. Spiritual Stirrings in Russia

FOR MANY YEARS I had made a habit of visiting a certain bookshop in Art Theater Street. This was not the big new bookstore. Nor was it the sprawling secondhand store where I liked to look for volumes about old Moscow. This was a store that specialized in political propaganda, and it was the place I went to find what lines the Agit-Prop section of the Central Committee was pushing. It was also a good place to see which members of the Presidium were depicted on the posters offered for sale. It was, in a word, a first-class barometer of ideological and political trends.

In the winter of 1962 there were two kinds of books and pamphlets which commanded big display. One dealt with space science, rocketry, Gagarin and Titov. This was expected and required no interpretation. The other had to do with religion—or, more properly, antireligion—and was somewhat surprising to me. I had never seen so big a display. There was a whole table devoted to antireligious materials, most of them fresh off the press and often of a quality considerably higher than the crude, defamatory potboilers with which I was familiar. The new propaganda was more apt to present a scientific explanation of the nature of the world than to heap abuse on the Old Testament or present elaborate denials that such a person as Christ had ever lived.

It had been apparent for some time that the question of religion had deeply troubled the party ideologues. There were two reasons for this. In the first place, despite the fact that Communist rule had prevailed in Russia for forty-five years, despite the general rise in enlightenment and literacy, and despite intensive antireligious campaigns and harassment of the church and its servants, Russia was still far from being the godless, atheistic, materialistic society which was the goal of the Marxist dogmatists. And, what was even more exasperating to the party faithful, there were signs aplenty that in the years since World War II there had been a resurgence of religious strength not only on the party of the dominant Russian Orthodox Church but by the smaller faiths as well and, particularly, by the Baptist Church.

This confronted the party with a whole series of problems. The persistence and stubbornness with which Russian people clung to their faith seemed to aggressive party specialists to constitute an affront to the Communist movement, implying a devotion deeper than could be commanded by the party. And the existence of church organizations was a special worry to those party officials concerned with security problems. This was not merely a consideration in drives against the Jewish or Roman Catholic faiths, each of which had obvious links abroad. It was considered to be a factor with respect to some of the smaller evangelical bodies. In the case of the Russian Orthodox Church it seemed to some party figures that the church was acquiring once again too much

[76]

strength. Might it not menace or challenge in some fashion the position or prestige of the party?

These questions did not appear to concern Khrushchev so much as they did some of his associates. Khrushchev showed a comfortable familiarity with the Orthodox Church. Although he described himself as a nonbeliever and even as an atheist, he showed no bashfulness about using God's name. He sprinkled his speeches and conversation with the familiar small change of the Russian believer's vocabulary. He knew his Bible, obviously had been taken to church as a youngster and could speak with the faithful in their own tongue. There was no sign that he had the slightest worry whether the Russian people went to church or not, and on at least one occasion he had personally intervened to warn some of his more aggressive associates against invoking force and invective against the church and its members.

But Khrushchev's attitude did not find much reflection at the operative party level. On this level I found in 1962 a vigor being applied to the struggle against the church which I had not seen in my previous experience in Russia.

The truth was that Stalin had virtually abandoned the fight against religion in the later years of his rule. He signed what amounted to a concordat with the old Patriarch Sergius September 4, 1943, during World War II. Under its terms the Orthodox Church pledged full support of the Soviet war effort. In return Stalin dissolved the League of the Godless, suspended the monthly *Atheists' Journal* and turned over its printing presses and paper to Sergius, who promptly began to turn out a *Monthly Journal of the Patriarchy*.

The end of the war saw no change. Many Russians had been brought back into the church by the war. Now, as villages petitioned the government for permission to reopen long-closed churches, the Kremlin gave its approval. By the time of Stalin's death new churches were being built in many villages where the old ones long since had been destroyed. Seminaries and religious academies were being re-established. The church was rapidly improving its position, materially, financially and spiritually.

The gains for the church were most impressive. At the time of the Revolution the church had numbered about 46,000 parishes and claimed a membership of nearly 100,-000,000. By 1943 the number of parishes had dropped to one-tenth the pre-Revolutionary figure, and there was no accurate estimate of membership. By early 1962 membership had been restored to about 50,000,000—roughly one-quarter of the population—and there were more than 20,000 churches and parishes and possibly 3,000 unorganized parishes, centered around houses of prayer. There were 73 dioceses and more than 60 monasteries and convents. Moscow had about 55 churches (in contrast to 600 before the Revolution) and Leningrad 15 as compared with 90.

It was this amazing recuperative power of the church which seriously concerned the party. Religion stubbornly refused to die out.

The stacks of antireligious books which I saw in the bookstore on Art Theater Street were the product of a decision by the party taken at the Twenty-first Congress in January, 1959, to revitalize its campaign against the persistence of religious faith. It was frank recognition by the party of the fact that religion had broadened the basis of its appeal—that it was no longer represented by the stereotype of the icon-kissing, superstitious old crone—that had caused the change in the content of antireligious literature. The new magazine, for example, *Science and Religion,* was an appeal to the logical instincts of educated man. It was a far cry from the ludicrous antireligious parades and song-chanting for which the schoolchildren of the first revolutionary generation were enlisted.

But the party was leaving nothing to chance. Although Khrushchev had warned in November, 1954, against the use of force against the church and its believers and called for respect of religious beliefs, these admonitions were now being honored mostly in the breach.

In Siberia just before the Twenty-second Party Congress local authorities in small communities closed the churches. In other places gangs of Young Communist bullyboys attacked churches, stoning windows, desecrating altars, pulling down icons and heaping abuse on the believers.

The attacks became so frequent that higher officials were alarmed. In some towns Komsomol druzhina units (which may have been responsible for the trouble in the first place) were ordered out to protect the churches. Local authorities were told the government did not wish to close churches by arbitrary means because of fear the believers would be driven underground. When evangelical faiths like the Seventh-day Adventists and Jehovah's Witnesses had been outlawed they had proliferated widely in the dark provinces beyond the Volga, in the fashion of the Orthodox sects of the nineteenth century, although on a far smaller scale. Confronted with a choice between a public church and an underground sect, the authorities preferred the public institution. It was much easier to keep an eye on.

The source of the attacks on the Orthodox Church was the same as that which inspired the rumors of party action against private property, ownership of automobiles and dachas. Rumors were circulated that the Twenty-second Party Congress would forbid religious institutions. These reports stemmed from actual proposals strongly advocated by the neo-Stalinists. In the provinces it was natural that officials supposed this public talk meant that the Congress would act along the same line. They simply sought to show their zealousness by closing down the churches before—not after—the party decrees.

The action in Siberia—and in some other areas of Russia—gave rise to rumors outside the country that the government had launched a general campaign to close Orthodox institutions. This was only partially true. Three Orthodox seminaries were closed, leaving five seminaries and two academies in operation. Two archbishops were sent to prison on charges of misappropriation of funds, nonpayment of taxes and other fiscal irregularities.

How many churches were closed could not be ascertained with certainty. Western estimates that the number was fifteen hundred to two thousand were not supported by Orthodox Church sources inside the country. But there had been many closings in western Russia, particularly in regions incorporated into the Soviet Union after World War II.

The famous Pechersky Monastery in Kiev was shut, but probably not for antireligious causes. In the spring of 1961 there was a calamitous earthslide in the Dnieper River cliffs, causing several hundred deaths. The area was sealed off, including the monastery and many ancient churches, while an investigation of possible further landslides was made.

But there was nervousness among church officials. For example, Metropolitan Nikolai died in December, 1961, and was buried with full honors of the church. Some foreign clergymen, in Moscow on their way home from the World Church Congress in New Delhi, were invited to the funeral.

One church official commented: "It is fortunate there were foreigners here. Otherwise there would have been rumors about Nikolai."

He was not wrong. I had heard rumors about Nikolai's death. One report said he had received improper medical treatment. The rumor was much the same as those involved in the famous "doctors' plot" of the days just before Stalin's death in which a group of Kremlin physicians were alleged to have caused the death of high party leaders by prescribing the wrong medicines and treatment.

The rumors about Nikolai were linked with his abrupt resignation in 1961 and his replacement by the thirty-two-year-old Archbishop Nicodemus, who had been his deputy. However, persons who had known Nikolai well insisted that he had often offered his resignation in the past; that the church had determined to make a change in foreign policy; that a change in personnel was dictated and that he had been offered the metropolitanship of Leningrad but instead had determined to go into retirement.

The whole subject of Nikolai was linked with the most interesting and significant turn in the affairs of the Russian Orthodox Church which had occurred in many years.

Nicodemus, who took over the church's department of foreign affairs from the brilliant Nikolai, was symbolic of the course which had emerged in the ancient church as a new generation of young priests, the first really new generation trained since the Bolshevik Revolution, had begun to assume important posts.

These men, all in their late twenties or early thirties, were seeking to break the image of the Orthodox Church as a fortress of superstition and backwardness. They were seeking to develop an appeal to youth. They were aware of the changing nature of the society in which they lived and of the rise of science and technology. They hoped to adapt their church to the complexity of the modern world. Like the ministers of Western churches, they wished to relate the church more intimately to the life of the community.

This was not easy in ecclesiastic terms because the Orthodox Church never underwent a Reformation. It had retained its liturgy, its forms, its ceremonials in almost untouched purity from premedievel times. Despite these handicaps the young men were tackling the problem boldly and unconventionally.

I found, for example, one priest presenting a series of sermons on topics of current and contemporary interest. He announced his series in advance, like a lecture course, and encouraged discussion after the sermon. Nothing like this normally had been done by the Orthodox Church.

The priest picked subjects that would be of intellectual interest to men and women of his congregation. He found that young people began to be attracted to the services in addition to the old women who had made up 80 percent of the congregation. Other churches were introducing activities especially interesting to young people—sports programs, football teams, hobbies.

In the field of international ecclesiastic policy Archbishop Nicodemus reversed the course followed by Nikolai. Nikolai had sought to gather all the Orthodox churches of the world under the dominance of the Moscow patriarchy. The policy of unification and Russification was roughly the equivalent of the Stalinist foreign policy in the period in which Nikolai rose to his power.

Nikolai had worked very closely and effectively with the late Georgi G. Karpov, chairman of the State Committee for Orthodox Church Affairs. Before assuming this post Karpov had been a leading figure in atheistic propaganda work. Nikolai was a commanding personality and it was long said— probably with accuracy—that he was able to dominate Karpov and win many concessions for the church.

Karpov's successor, Vladimir Kuroiedov, was a much more vigorous official.

The new young men of the church were carrying out a foreign policy line based on ecumenical relations as widespread and close as possible with other churches. Thus, for the first time the Orthodox Church joined the World Council of Churches (after many years in which Nikolai delivered scathing attacks against its activities). It was seeking closer fraternal relations with other Orthodox Church groups and with the Church of England. While the historic antagonism between the Moscow Patriarchy and the Papacy could hardly be said to have lessened, there was a lightening of emphasis on attacks against the Vatican.

It may have been coincidental, but parallel to this the Soviet party press diminished its propaganda assault against the Vatican and for the first time the Kremlin and the Vatican formally exchanged greetings.

The religious situation increasingly reflected an awareness of the changing nature of the world. Both the party and the church might have been said to have gotten out of step with the pace of events—the party with its primitive, ritualistic attacks on "wonder-working" icons and the church with its devotion to form and ritual.

But what of the people? Here I found something possibly more significant than anything in the realm of either party or church. Within the most advanced echelon of Soviet science —or so I was informed—there had emerged a tendency to seek a nonmaterialist concept of the universe. This development had shocked conventionally minded Communist party functionaries. For some of the most brilliant men in Soviet Russia, men whose minds had given the nation her great achievements in physics, in space, in nuclear technology, were now suggesting that there must exist in the universe a force or power superior to any concept born of man's mind.

I was not able to establish how widespread this tendency

95 n

was. Names were not being given—for obvious reasons. But I was told that eminent men in the galaxy of astronomers, mathematicians and advanced theorists were involved. These were men of influence, and their beliefs were not likely to be confined for long within their own specialized fields. They had not become believers in formal religion nor in religious dogma. Their faith was akin to that which was shared by many of their Western scientific colleagues. What was vital was that these men no longer subscribed to the atheism dictated by Marx and the party.

As one of these men was said to have formulated his belief: "I do not believe in some religious catechism. But I do believe —as a scientist—that there is a force within the universe which is superior to that of man. Perhaps some might call this God."

One of the most gifted of the younger Soviet writers, V. Tendryakov, summarized this kind of belief in a recent short story. He put it like this:

"I do not imagine God as He is depicted on icons. To me God is a sort of spiritual principle, the stimulus to the emergence of the galaxies, the stars, the planets and of everything which lives and reproduces on these planets, from the most elementary cells up to man."

For men of such tendencies the primitive belief of the church and the primitive nonbelief of the party were insufficient. What was now going forward in Russia, it seemed quite plain, was the first phase of a struggle between party and church for the faith of the most brilliant figures of contemporary society. Once again I found within the framework of the Soviet system a contest of opposing concepts—not of surface ideas but of ideals and theories which went to the heart of the Western way of thought. In the field of religion there were deep stirrings, stirrings as fundamental as Russia had ever known.

Alongside these there were other, more simple stirrings—the rise of the Baptist Church, for instance, which was demonstrating an appeal to young people which might be envied by their coreligionists in America. The Baptists, with some 600,-000 members in Russia, were probably the fastest-growing church in the Soviet Union. And the vigor of this growth had, inevitably, caused the party to react forcibly—particularly in the propaganda sphere. The newspapers of the Communist Youth League were constantly publishing articles by ex-Baptists, exposing the alleged sins of the church. They were supposed to divert young people from their studies and encourage them in various kinds of superstition.

Although the Baptists were known throughout the Soviet union as being good, moral, sober, hard-working people, articles were published about deacons getting drunk and running off with the Sunday offerings.

This kind of pressure did not leave the Baptist Church entirely unaffected. There was a slight drop in the number of baptisms and weddings in Moscow and Leningrad. Some small churches in rural areas were closed. Others found themselves up against campaigns conducted by local authorities. But they were weathering the storm without too much trouble.

The worst abuse was directed against the Jehovah's Witnesses and Seventh-day Adventists. In Moldavia four persons were sentenced to death and fifteen others were given prison sentences for the murder of a "nonbeliever." In Kirghizia three Volga German families were deprived of parental rights over their children on grounds they refused to let them go to school on Saturdays or join the Pioneer youth organization. The families were Seventh-day Adventists.

The trial was conducted in bullying fashion. The audience was encouraged to boo the defendants and cheer the verdict and the newspaper commented: "Henceforth, Soviet parents will be the loving and caring educators of these children and the time will come when the children will cordially thank them for their trouble." Sergei Pavlov, head of the young Communist movement, told the Komsomol Congress in April, 1962, that freedom of religion did not extend to minor children. The minds of the young, he insisted, must be kept free of religious contamination.

In Lithuania two priests of the Roman Catholic Church were sentenced to prison on charges of involvement in a plot to embezzle funds and use church property for their own purposes.

If—after more than forty years of experience—the party could think of no more effective anti-religious tactics than those of the street bully and state persecution it did not seem likely to me that Communism was likely to "solve" the religious problem in the near future. The church and its formal institutions could, obviously, be harassed as they had been so often in the past. But the flame of belief which burned in man's breast would never be put out by propaganda, police or street rowdies. Indeed, the very use of such tactics seemed an anachronism. More an admission of futility than genuine determination to stamp the mark of atheism on the new generation.

I might be wrong, but it appeared to me that young Archbishop Nicodemus and his fellow priests of the new generation came much closer to being in tune with the emerging spirit of Russia than the Agit-Prop brigades and their allies in the local bureaucracy.

7. Mongolia Turns West

THE HIGH PLATEAUS and steep mountain valleys seemed to sleep under their winter blanket of snow just as in the days of Genghis Khan. From the low-flying plane I could see a herd of horses or a flock of sheep, here and there, black dots against the sparkling white, grazing in the lowland pastures. From tiny clusters of *yurts* thin columns of blue smoke rose straight upward in the still sunshine and cloudless Mongolian sky.

Returning after an absence of two and a half years I saw few signs of change in the snow-white world of the endless countryside. True, there was a new Russian-style airport building and, even from the air, I could see that much construction had gone up in Ulan Bator since my last visit in the summer of 1959.

But as I flew south from Irkutsk in the small, Russian-built, Mongol-operated Ilyushin-14, the jagged mountains, the black forests and the broad steppe were clothed in timeless tranquillity.

[87]

At the airport the landscape was gay with the bright scarlet, purples, greens and golden yellows of the winter *dels*. The del was the traditional Mongol gown, one of the warmest garments ever invented. Inside it was sheepskin from neck to ankle, or, sometimes, red fox. Outside it was usually covered in gay silks. Both men and women wore the del. By tradition the men wore bright yellow, green or red sashes, called *bous*. The women did not in ancient times—although many now did. Thus, the Mongol name for man is *bousteichud* and for woman *bousguidhud,* meaning "with sash" and "without sash."

I was met by a tall, serious Mongol named Purudorj. As we waited for my bags to clear customs we made casual conversation. I asked if he had ever been in China. No, he said, he had not.

"China has very many people," Purudorj said. His English was halting and much of our conversation was in Russian. "They have almost 700 million people."

"China has almost as many people as Russia, America and India all together," I said. "And by 1975 they will have more than one billion."

"That is a very great number of people," Mr. Purudorj said. "Very great."

It was curious, I thought, that my first conversation after landing in Mongolia should come right to the heart of what was probably the most significant political fact in Asia—the massive weight of China's population. Mr. Purudorj did not attempt to draw any conclusion from this fact but he did not seem to derive any pleasure from China's monstrous statistics.

I asked Mr. Purudorj about the man who had been my guide in 1959, an ardent advocate of Chinese Communism who hotly had insisted that China's way was the best way

for Mongolia and, indeed, for all Asia. I had heard much talk
of that kind in Ulan Bator during the summer of 1959. Most
of the young Mongols I talked with then had been to China.
They were impressed. I was impressed too, at the great effort
that China was making to woo Mongolia. It was here that I
saw for the first time open competition between the Soviet
and Chinese Communisms for the favor of an Asian people.
Mr. Purudorj informed me that my former guide had now
gone to China. When he might return was not known.

Ulan Bator in 1959 had swarmed with Chinese—members
of a labor and technical force which numbered perhaps 25,-
000 or more, sent into Mongolia as free assistance by the
Chinese. I puzzled over China's generosity until I learned
that the Mongols had given the Chinese the option of becoming Mongol citizens and settling on the land—if they wished
—once the aid projects were completed. It was, I suspected,
a device to shoehorn a Chinese minority into Mongolia
which, later, might be used as the nucleus of a fifth column
when, as and if China felt powerful enough to try to take
over the country.

As we drove into town along the snowy highway I wondered which power had come out on top in the struggle—
China or Russia? Two years ago there had been thousands of
Chinese working along this road, putting up apartment
houses, erecting factories, constructing a bridge, widening
the pavement, installing sewers, water mains, electric con-
duits.

Today I found them vanished. Construction work was still
going on but most of the projects the Chinese had worked
on were completed. There were whole areas of the city which
had been transformed. Crossing the Tul River by the new
steel-and-concrete bridge I could see that the "battleground,"
as I had called the center of town (in the summer of 1959 it

was so torn up with construction that it looked like a city being prepared for street fighting), had disappeared. Gone were the great camps of Chinese workers, located a stone's throw from Sukhe Bator Square. We rode over broad boulevards to an imposing, modern building. It was the Ulan Bator Hotel, gleaming with modern decor from the plate-glass doors to the sunlighted suites, furnished in the latest Scandinavian taste.

Two years before I had stayed at a pleasant but primitive "guest house"—a refurbished barracks some ten miles out in the country. There was no place in town that had plumbing or running water. Now I was provided with a suite and private bath with excellent plumbing—better, indeed, than in my Moscow hotel.

That night I watched a bunch of youngsters from Karakorum, the ancient capital of Genghis Khan, jitterbugging in the hotel restaurant to the music of "Frank's Band." Frank's band was an eight-piece jazz combo made up of four saxophones, two trumpets, a bass viol and a drummer. They had glitter shields, a drum that glowed red and green from within and a repertoire of American numbers that included "Sugar Puss, I Love You So." The repertoire was courtesy of "Music U. S. A.," the famous American short-wave all-music radio program. But the glitter shields and instruments had come with the hotel along with the new plumbing, Swedish-type furniture, beautiful porcelein, specially blown glassware and silverware—all from Czechoslovakia. The hotel was planned, directed and managed by Czechs (but built with Chinese labor). The Mongols were learning the hotel business under Czech guidance.

Change—I found it everywhere I went in Ulan Bator. But it was not merely physical. A new spirit seemed at work among the people—the intellectuals, ordinary factory workers and even the herdsmen who still warmed themselves around the iron stoves of the yurts in the winter pasture lands.

Breaking out of a cocoon of long isolation the Mongols were working hard to broaden their national horizons and to forge economic, cultural and diplomatic ties with other countries.

One Mongol after another, bursting with shy pride, said to me, "You know, we have people in New York now—at the United Nations."

Mongolia had taken her seat at the United Nations only a few weeks before my arrival and in the minds of her citizens this event was symbolic of the new Mongolia, a proud and prestigious development.

This was only a first step. Next, or so believed the Mongols, from the Acting Premier, Lvsantserengiin Tsende, on down, would come the establishment of diplomatic relations with the United States.

"We're all learning English," a professor at Ulan Bator University chuckled. "Everyone I know is hoping to visit the United States."

"Do you think that America might let a group of our journalists pay a visit—even before diplomatic relations are established?" an editor inquired hopefully.

"Would it be very expensive to publish a magazine about Mongolia in the United States?" an official asked. "We're so anxious for the American people to learn about our country."

Repeatedly, the Mongols expressed appreciation for United States action in helping Mongolia at long last to enter the United Nations. Because I was an American they wanted to show their feelings to me. Some Mongols seemed to believe that the United States had sponsored Mongolia's admission.

I found Mr. Tsende disappointed but philosophical about

America's failure to establish diplomatic relations after opening up discussion in the summer of 1961. Mr. Tsende appeared to be aware that there was strong official U.S. sentiment for this step and that it had been balked only because of difficulties raised by the Nationalist Chinese government.

Mr. Tsende, a strapping, six-foot Mongolian with a wide smile and a strong handclasp, was the No. 2 man in Ulan Bator. The Premier, Mr. Tsedenbal, was absent in Moscow at the time of my visit. Mr. Tsende was careful to emphasize that there was no obstacle from the Mongol side so far as relations were concerned. He felt the United States could play a positive role in Mongolia's future—not only in trade, artistic and cultural exchanges, but in providing Mongolia with technical and scientific know-how, especially in agriculture and livestock breeding.

"We know," he said, "that in your American West you have conditions which in many respects are similar to our own. We are eager to have the benefit of American techniques."

It was obvious that Mongolia was seeking to broaden her contacts with nations outside the Communist community. While Mr. Tsende emphasized that Mongolia's relations with Communist China had not so far been affected by the broadening Soviet-Chinese conflict I could not avoid the conclusion that Mongolia looked to the future through westward glasses. Mr. Tsende revealed that more than 75 percent of Mongolia's outside aid was now coming from Russia and only 20 percent from China. The Soviet predominance was due to rise sharply in the 1961-65 Mongolian five-year plan. Mr. Tsende said there were still ten to twelve thousand Chinese in Mongolia.

"Where are they?" I inquired. "I have seen hardly any."

Mr. Tsende smiled. "The weather is very cold. Perhaps they are all working indoors."

The airplane which had brought me east from Moscow had been filled with Bulgarians and Bulgarian wives and children, coming out to work in Mongolia. Mr. Tsende said there had been a marked increase in technical aid from Eastern Europe and that many Bulgarians were arriving to work on construction and agricultural projects. I wondered whether the Bulgarians might be coming as replacements in case the Chinese withdrew.

In fact, I was not entirely convinced that the Chinese had not already left until one day we drove across the broad plain four or five miles outside Ulan Bator. I noticed in the distance a familiar sight. Just after Stalin's death I had made a long trip into eastern Siberia and became accustomed to the appearance of labor camps which dotted the area. What I saw across the plain looked much the same—the same high wooden fence, topped by strands of barbed wire, rows of small huts inside and at each corner a high wooden watchtower with tommy gunners. The only difference was that these huts had a curious kind of thatched roof, lashed down with tarpaulins. There were three camps scattered across the open plain.

"What are those establishments?" I asked the Mongol who was with me.

"Those are for the Chinese workers," he replied.

I never learned whether the tommy gunners were Mongols watching to see that the Chinese didn't leave or Chinese eying their own people lest they make a break. But an end obviously had come to free and easy mingling of the Chinese with the Mongols. No longer did the Chinese swarm through the center of the city. No longer did they ride their bicycles along the river. I saw not a single Chinese at the theater and only a handful in the stores and markets.

One day all Ulan Bator turned out at the airport for the

arrival of the Soviet spaceman Major Gherman Titov and his pretty wife. The whole town buzzed. The streets were decorated with red Soviet banners and red-blue-yellow Mongol flags. Factories closed. Schoolchildren were let out. But there wasn't a Chinese at the airport—except for the Ambassador—and along the line of march Chinese labor crews patiently went ahead digging ditches and laying sewer pipes. The only Chinese who watched the parade were four men who leaned on long-handled shovels and looked on with curious but guilty expressions as though they knew they shouldn't be neglecting their urgent shovel work.

It was no accident, of course, that these changes had come about. I found not a single Chinese patient in the leading hospital (although there were perhaps thirty Russians, Czechs, Germans and Bulgarians undergoing treatment). There was only one Chinese faculty member at Ulan Bator University —a language teacher—and about twenty Chinese language students. At a big textile center which I had watched going up in 1959 under the guidance of Chinese engineers there were only half a dozen Chinese left. The chief lama of the Mongol Buddhists reported that for the third year running they had been cut off from their Buddhist coreligionists in Tibet, unable to make the customary pilgrimages because of a ban by the Chinese government. Mongol scientists told me there had been a sudden and total interruption in contact with their colleagues in Chinese-controlled Inner Mongolia.

"One Chinese told me they were unable to send us their journals because of lack of paper," a Mongol scientist told me. "But most of the paper in our stores comes from China."

In the Mongol stores I found Chinese consumer goods— Dragon Column sugar, Three Star crayons, Golden Dragon thermos bottles, Red Poppy candies and Heavenly Blossom tea.

But the heavy weight of Mongolia's economic system had swung to the Soviet side and this was what counted. Russia had won the first round of the contest with China for dominant influence in Mongolia and she had done it by pumping in hundreds of millions of rubles in loans and grants. China had literally been backed into the corner.

The cost of this had not been small. For example, the 1961-65 plan called for a total expenditure of 4.5 billion *togruks.* The togruk is nominally valued at 4.55 to the dollar and 4.45 to the ruble. The rate is anomalous because in Moscow the ruble is valued at 1.11 to the dollar.

The Soviet is providing at least 14 percent of the cost of the Mongol five-year plan, China 4 percent and other Communist countries 2 or 3 percent. Over the five years the Soviet contribution was calculated at $350 million, or about $350 per head on the basis of a Mongolian population estimated at below one million. China's investment would be $50 million. Total Soviet investment in Mongolia by 1965 would come to $975 million—if not more—compared with Chinese advances of $115 million.

The magnitude of the Soviet effort was brought out by comparison with, for example, United States aid to Iran. In the same peroid U.S. aid to Iran ran only about 25 percent more than total Communist aid to Mongolia (just under $1.5 billion) but Iran's population was twenty times that of Mongolia.

Where two years ago China seemed to be challenging Soviet influence in Mongolia successfully, now the tide ran in the other direction. Mongolia's Soviet-trained, Soviet-educated leaders had come down firmly on Russia's side of the Chinese-Soviet conflict. Mr. Tsende emphatically told me that Mongolia had no intention of emulating China's commune system. They were developing their own approach to agricultural problems—an approach remarkably like that of the Soviet Union. The Mongol leaders hoped to receive Chinese help as long as possible but they were publicly proclaiming their support for Moscow in the great ideological quarrel. Unlike the Communist leaders of North Korea and North Vietnam, the Mongol spokesmen were not trying to carry water on both shoulders. Alone among the Asian Communist parties the Mongols had denounced Albania in terms as sweeping as the Kremlin's.

Two years ago Mongols talked with pride and enthusiasm of trips to Peking and contacts with China. Now I found that unless I brought up the subject China was seldom mentioned. I asked about aid projects. Officials spoke of the Soviet Union, Czechoslovakia, Germany. What about China? Oh, yes. China, too.

A professional man told me with enthusiasm of a trip he had recently taken to Japan. "Did you pass through China?" I asked. "Oh, yes," he said. "I had a most interesting visit in Hong Kong." "What about Peking?" "Well, I didn't stop there."

The whole focus of Mongolian interest seemed to have changed. The men with whom I talked spoke with pride of commercial ties with Switzerland or England. A Japanese delegation had recently been in Ulan Bator, and outside of the United States it seemed that Japan was the non-Communist nation toward which the Mongols were most attracted.

"Japan is an Asian state," one Mongol engineer said. "But her standard of life is higher than that of many European countries. It is very impressive."

Along with the rising interest in the West and the non-Communist world I found the atmosphere of Ulan Bator notably relaxed since my visit in 1959. Visitors from the West were still a great event. But much of the suspicion seemed to have vanished. Many intellectuals mentioned their pride and pleasure at visits from such Americans as Justice William O. Douglas and Owen Lattimore.

"It used to be impossible to get books and publications or even mail from the West," one scholar told me. "Now it is all different. We write back and forth and books are beginning to come in."

On his paper-littered desk I saw three recent letters from the United States—one from Michigan, one from Kansas and and one from New York. None of them had yet been answered.

If there were any special security precautions in effect in Ulan Bator I did not see them—except in the case of the Chinese labor force. When I went to the big government office building on Sukhe Bator Square to visit Mr. Tsende there was only one doorman-guard on duty. And I watched the Acting Premier mix casually in a crowd of several thousand persons at the Ulan Bator Airport. If there was a plain-clothes men with him I could not spot him. However, security details accompanied the Soviet and Chinese Ambassadors.

Stalin had not been quite downgraded when I left Mongolia in December, 1961, but he was not the great figure he had been two years before. His statue stood outside the Academy of Science building but his name had been dropped from the building's title. In one of the two Ulan Bator bookstores I found stacks of Stalin pictures on sale. The other store had a big stack of Premier Khrushchev's. Neither one carried pictures of Premier Tsedenbal.

The heart of Ulan Bator is Sukhe Bator Square—an expanse of asphalt somewhat larger than Red Square in Moscow. In the square stands a mausoleum, a smaller replica of that in Red Square. In the mausoleum rested the bodies of two Mongol Communist leaders—Sukhe Bator, the revolutionary figure who with the aid of the Soviet Red Army seized power in Mongolia in 1921, and Choibalsan, who succeeded him and ruled until his death in Moscow in 1952.

Shortly after I left Mongolia Premier Tsedenbal returned from his long stay in Moscow. One of his first acts was to deliver a speech attacking Choibalsan for ruling Mongolia in much the same dictatorial fashion as Stalin had ruled Russia. His speech was parallel to Khrushchev's fresh assault on Stalin at the Twenty-second Party Congress. Would Mongolia now take the next logical step and follow Moscow's lead by opening up her mausoleum and removing the body of Choibalsan?

In one area I found that repression in Mongolia had not ceased. This concerned the Buddhist faith. The elderly Abbot Erdenepil had retired as chief of the great Gandantehchinling Monastery and his place had been assumed by a man named U. Gombojav, who was a member of the Academy of Science as well as nominal chief of the church. His function seemed principally to maintain contact with Buddhists of other countries. He had recently returned from Cambodia. But within his own country he admitted that the faith was withering away. There were still ten thousand lamas in Mongolia but only two temples, the Gandantehchinling and one at Dormrode. There were one hundred monks at Gandantehchinling and forty at Dormrode. The others had no temples.

"My father and mother are still firm believers," an intellectual told me. "Most people in the country still believe."

But it was difficult to see how Buddhism could long survive without new priests and places of worship.

When I talked about this with the Reverend Gombojav he became irritated.

"In Mongolia there is full freedom to worship or not to worship," he insisted.

"But what about the future?" I asked.

"I can't say what the future of Buddhism will be," he said, "but I hope it will live long and help the people to live a happy, useful and peaceful life."

Apparently he perceived my skepticism.

"And what can you tell us," he said suddenly, "about the Buddhists in America. What is the future of the Buddhist Church in America?"

When I told him of the rising interest among Americans in Zen Buddhism he was plainly surprised.

On my earlier trip to Mongolia I had found the country just launching a great program to put the plow to her vast virgin grasslands, the great green grazing areas which had nourished Mongolia's horses (and sheep) since the time of Genghis Khan. I had been concerned over the program. It seemed to me that the Russian authors of the plow-the-land scheme might turn one of the most magnificent livestock regions in Asia into a dustbowl.

Acting Premier Tsende was at some pains to correct this impression. He said that Mongolia had no intention of over-turning her traditional economy. What was hoped was to raise enough grain and fodder to give the country a better reserve for winter and a measure of diversification.

Thus far some 600,000 hectares had been plowed and the total was due to double by 1965. Grain production rose to 256,000 metric tons in 1960 but was down sharply in 1961 due to drought. Livestock totals were down, too—10 percent since 1940. Cattle were down 30 percent and sheep 20 percent.

One brilliant cold day when the sun blazed in the faded blue of the winter sky I drove out into the country to see for myself. It was clear that it was the countryside which could make or break Mongolia's future.

Outside Ulan Bator I found a winter wonderland. Herds of cattle and sheep grazed on grain stubble, the stubble gleaming golden yellow against the light snow cover. Straw, hay and feed grasses lay in scattered mows. Stocks of feed were piled high in the winter corrals.

I had thought that the yurt, the Mongolian conical felt tent, must be a deadly place in the 40 degree below zero cold which is common on the Mongolian steppe. I could not have been more mistaken. Inside the yurt of Herdsman Handa of the Zamt collective farm it was so warm that his two little girls played half-naked on the earth floor where the grass was still green. He and his wife doffed their winter dels as they offered me *buz*, or Mongolian ravioli, and winter tea—the normal "five elements" beverage of water, salt, butter, milk and tea to which fried flour had been added by way of strengthening.

To Handa the winter was the best time of the year. This was the season when he went into the nearby foothills hunting *yneg* or red foxes, *tarvga* or marmots and *gahai* or wild pigs. He got 5.70 togruks a skin for marmots. There was a fine red fox skin drying from the ridgepole of his yurt. He proudly showed me his fuzzy-furred Mongol pony and his hand-made sled with curved wooden runners. He was a section leader at the co-op and had five families under his direction. For four years he had belonged to the co-op and while he had only three cows and a horse as against thirty animals when he was a private herdsman he figured his income was considerably more.

We drove further into the interior. There were few vehicles, except for occasional trucks carrying oil or coal, moving over the frosty highway. I thought the temperature was about 20 below but the Mongols said it was nearer to 40 below but so dry and windless that it seemed warmer. Finally at Jargalant, northwest of Ulan Bator, I found some three thousand Mongols engaged in a state farm complex which provided a pattern of what Mongolia's leaders hoped their future agriculture would resemble.

On a 440,000-acre spread about 100,000 acres was under cultivation, half in wheat, the rest largely in fodder or fallow land. There were forty thousand animals on the farm, half of them sheep. Among the forty thousand animals were two Przhevalsky horses, one of the rarest of wild horse breeds, first seen and identified by the famous Russian explorer, Nikolai Przhevalsky, in the nineteenth century. Only a few hundred of these animals survived in the wilds of southwest Mongolia. At the Jargalant farm the *tahi,* as they were called, were being crossbred with Mongol and Russian blood lines. They were extremely fast and sturdy. The stud director told me they were nearly twice as fast as ordinary horses.

In the cozy yurts, in the chilly collective farm offices, in the country guest houses there was one all-consuming topic of conversation: the weather. It was not the cold which dropped well below 40 degrees in the course of my trip which most concerned the Mongol countrymen. It was the snow. The snow was deep—very deep, they agreed. To me the three or four inches which lay on the rolling hillsides did not seem deep but a herdsman explained: "It isn't that the snow is deep for us—it is the cattle we worry about. To us a deep snow is one which covers the grass or stubble so the animals cannot eat. First, we must think of our animals. Without them we could not live."

This was the problem—the stabilization of livestock feed —which the Mongol officials placed highest among the goals of their land reforms.

There was another goal as well. For centuries Mongolia had been a nomadic land. Her people followed the animals to the high plateaus in summer and back down to the lowlands in winter. This had been the pattern of Mongol life since long before Genghis Khan. Even today it was little changed.

But now, at least so far as Mongolia's youth was concerned, it was going to be broken. So Acting Premier Tsende told me. Only by breaking it, he was convinced, could Mongolian youth be educated and trained for the technology of the modern world. In fifteen years—if Mongolia continued to get the massive aid she was now receiving—her leaders hoped to raise her living standards to something approximating those of Europe, Eastern Europe at any rate. For this Mongolia needed trained, skilled young people—not another generation of shepherds and horsemen, wise to the saddle but ignorant of letters and the machine.

"We are not going to let another generation of our young people grow up illiterate," Mr. Tsende said. "We are bringing an end to this. Now."

In the next few years a system of boarding schools would be set up. The older people would continue to accompany the animals on their inevitable treks. But the youngsters would stay behind and learn the skills of the modern world.

Change, deep, fundamental and swift, was moving across the Mongol steppe and with it the ancient pattern of Mongol life, which had not altered since the days of the Golden Horde, would inevitably and irrevocably be broken.

The inspiration for the transformation was coming from the West, not the East. Mongolia had chosen Russia, not China, and unless the United States rejected the opportunity there was going to be a role for America in Mongolia's future. What we made of this, I was convinced, depended more upon us than the Mongols. They were ready and eager to cooperate. We were still trying to make up our minds.

8. Moscow and Peking Choose Separate Paths

ONE NIGHT in late November the Yugoslav Embassy in Moscow held its annual reception. It was a glittering affair. More than two hundred Russians, including several members of the Communist Party Presidium, turned out. There were gaiety, laughter, toasts in champagne and vodka. Later in the evening there was dancing. Almost every ambassador in the city was present—except the Chinese. A young Chinese attaché explained that his ambassador was ill. So sorry.

There were two parties in Moscow that night. By chance Albania celebrates the same national day of liberation and there was a reception at the Albanian Embassy as well as at the Yugoslav. Twelve or fifteen Russians appeared and left after the compulsory thirty minutes. The top men were Georgi Zhukov, chairman of the Cultural Affairs Committee who had just failed of elevation to the party Central Committee, and Jacob Malik, the veteran Soviet diplomat who also had just been demoted. There was a sprinkling of East European diplomats, the Canadian Ambassador (who crashed the gates out of curiosity), a couple of correspondents who did the same thing and were welcomed warmly, the Danish Ambassador (whose country recognizes Albania, but who was not recognized by the porter at the door and had to show his diplomatic credentials), the Cuban Ambassador (who attends every reception in town) and fifteen or twenty Chinese—headed by the Chinese Ambassador, who seemed to have made a miraculous recovery.

The Albanians did their best to show their hospitality but somehow the party never got off the ground. Perhaps it was the beautiful white marble bust of Stalin which had a central place in the ballroom. The Russians had just removed Stalin from the Red Square Mausoleum and the presence of the bust, the ostentatious departure of the Russians, the precise smiles of the Chinese and embarrassing eagerness of the Albanians to welcome any strays cast a pall over the occasion.

It was only a week or ten days later that Soviet authorities ordered the Albanian mission to pack up and leave Moscow. About the same time a rumor was circulated that the Chinese were also going. This, however, proved only partially true. The staff had been reduced to half a dozen, the Ambassador had gone home, all Russian chauffeurs, cooks, maids, secretaries and interpreters had been fired, but the embassy in its vast compound on the outskirts of the city, far from any other diplomatic mission, stayed open.

There was another rumor in Moscow. This was to the effect that direct plane service between Moscow and Peking had been canceled. This, too, turned out to be an exaggeration. Service by the big TU-104 jets had been cut to twice weekly but the planes were running practically empty. There was also a small supplemental service between Irkutsk and Peking via Ulan Bator, provided by the Mongols and the

Chinese, using Soviet planes.

The curtailment of contacts between the Russians and the Chinese was obvious wherever you looked. The number of Chinese students at Leningrad and Moscow universities had been cut back. None whatever remained at provincial universities in Irkutsk and Tashkent. The special facilities which Intourist set up at the Irkutsk transit point to handle the large volume of Chinese traffic which I had seen only two years earlier were now virtually unused. Not more than one or two Chinese a week were coming through and in all of 1961 Irkutsk had seen only three groups of Chinese. The number of Japanese tourists in Irkutsk outnumbered the Chinese twenty-five to one and for the country as a whole Americans tourists outnumbered the Chinese by a far greater margin.

These events formed the small change of Moscow conversation in the winter of 1961-62 along with the inevitable stories:

"How do you classify movies?"

"Excellent, good, medium, bad and—Chinese."

Or:

Chou En-lai is walking a dog on the boulevard.

"What kind of a dog is that, Mr. Premier, a Pekingese?"

"No. An Albanian."

What was the meaning of the gossip and the stories? Simply this. Since the open breach between Moscow and Peking at the Communist party's Twenty-second Congress the Russians had—at least among themselves—abandoned all pretense that the conflict did not exist. The ordinary Russian made jokes about it. The journalists repeated the latest gossip. Even men high in the party frankly spoke about the difficulty of the Chinese and their inability to come to an understanding with them.

In the early stages of the conflict it had been quite different. In the summer of 1959 Soviet officials kept up the sham of good relations. This was no longer true. This was left to the Chinese side. Deputy Premier Chen Yi ostentatiously greeted Soviet concert stars when they came to Peking but there was no sign of reciprocity on the Soviet side. About all the Russians seemed willing to do was to publish one-inch or half-inch items in *Pravda* or *Izvestia*, reporting that ten thousand Chinese workers were attending evening school or that a steel mill brigade had exceeded its production quota.

But it was not just skirmishing. Deadly serious moves were being made. The Russians had withdrawn almost all of the thousands of technicians and engineers whom they had sent to China. The specialists had begun to come back in 1960 or even before. By early 1961 the withdrawal was almost complete. And when the specialists returned to Moscow they brought with them the blueprints for the projects on which they were working. Not only had China been deprived of skilled assistance. She was left in many cases without the detailed plans to complete the factories, dams, bridges and buildings which the Soviet was helping to construct.

Soviet shipments of machinery and installations to China were being continued on a reduced scale. The Russians had cut back their commitments, citing China's inability to pay (because of Peking's need of foreign exchange to purchase grain due to her crop failures). It was not uncommon, I was informed, for Soviet machines to arrive in apparently good order. But when the Chinese came to assemble them a vital part would be missing.

"What you do not realize," I was told by a man who had spent some time in China, "is that China is now subject to a double blockade. First there is yours. And now there is Russia's."

No longer was this a quarrel of words, a clash of dialectic arguments. The Russians had brought to bear upon their quondam allies the full weight of economic pressures, deliberately applied at a moment and in sectors where they would be felt most deeply.

Nor was it merely the pressure of Moscow—powerful as this was. Russia had allied behind her the support of the whole Eastern European economic bloc. All of the other Communist trading partners had swung into line. If the shoe pinched—and it did pinch—Peking would have to look beyond the Communist world for succor.

The Soviet offensive against China was not limited to economic weapons. Moscow had launched a global campaign to swing the weight of every Communist party in the world behind her position, to bring the full authority of the world movement to bear upon China, to isolate the Chinese from their natural Marxist allies.

The drive to align the world parties was well under way even before the walk-out of Premier Chou En-lai from the Twenty-second Party Congress had signaled to Communists everywhere that the breach had become irremediable. In the weeks before the opening of the session Mr. Khrushchev and his closest allies had worked over the chiefs of as many Communist parties as they could reach. The leaders of the East European parties were in Moscow again and again and at frequent intervals missions from Moscow were sent out to encourage the waverers such as Bulgaria.

By dint of enormous exertion Moscow had managed to line up all the European parties (of course, excepting Albania) for their side. In Asia they were not able to do so well. Flattery, persuasion, threats, enormous new grants of loans and credits—none of these tactics could win the North Koreans and the North Vietnamese over to full support of

Moscow. Kim ir Sen and Ho Chih Min were too close to China. The best Khrushchev could get was a wavering neutrality which clearly indicated a tendency to slip toward the Chinese side.

The drive to align the Communist world did not halt with the Twenty-second Party Congress. It went on with new intensity in the following period. The Chinese were working equally hard by this time to woo the uncommitted comrades to their way of thinking.

In the end geography appeared to be playing a more important role than arguments. The parties of Southeast Asia and of East Asia in general (excepting those loyal allies of Moscow, the Mongols) inclined more and more to the Chinese side despite the best efforts of the Kremlin.

What was notable was the total character of the struggle. In the typical fashion of Communists, once the quarrel had started it began to acquire an internal and seemingly inevitable momentum. It was reminiscent of the historic splits within the Marxist movement in the past—the breach between Marx and LaSalle, between Lenin and Plekhanov, between Stalin and Trotsky, between the Social Democrats and the Communists. No middle ground was being left. No area for compromise. And each Communist, whether he was an underground leader in a Latin-American dictatorship or the chief of a powerful West European legal party, was being required to stand up and be counted on one side or the other.

There had been three major efforts at a reconciliation of Moscow and Peking. There had been the 1957 meeting in Moscow which had produced a joint declaration signed by Russia, China and all the other parties represented (except the Yugoslavs). There had been a private meeting in Bucharest in 1960 and the public meeting in Moscow in November, 1960. Each meeting had brought a paper compromise, a *pro forma* declaration of unity which was violated by the principals to the dispute before the ink was hardly dry.

The chance that after the failure of all these efforts, after the increasingly vituperative exchanges (which almost led to fisticuffs at the December, 1961, plenary meeting of the World Peace Congress in Stockholm), after the public denunciation of Khrushchev and the Soviet leadership by Albania (and vice versa), any kind of binding truce could be patched up seemed remote.

What had brought the two great Communist empires to a parting of the ways?

There were more reasons than one. There was, it became obvious, a long history of secret bad blood between the two movements. The roots of the bad party relationship had been nurtured in the days of Stalin. It was probable that Stalin had never trusted Mao and had taken no pains to conceal this. It was probable that Stalin had rejected many a request for aid by Mao in the days when the Chinese Communists were fighting for their lives in the 1930's. It was possible that Stalin had urged them to compromise and subordinate themselves to Chiang Kai-shek at the end of World War II. It may well have been that Stalin sought to detach Manchuria from China after the rise of the Communists to power, utilizing the enigmatic Manchurian leader Kao Kang, whose mysterious suicide in 1954 had never been explained.

But none of this ancient history satisfactorily explained the inability of the two movements to get along within a framework of cooperating toward the common good. The reasons for this inability certainly lay in the present rather than in the past. Almost certainly a major factor was the contrast in the stages of economic development and social and political needs of the two big Communist states.

Before the Twenty-second Party Congress convened in Moscow Khrushchev drafted the grandiose outline of a twenty-year plan for the attainment of a living standard equal to or better than that of the United States. This was a blueprint of the Communist society which Moscow was striving to build. It was presented as a Soviet plan to be achieved by Soviet society. But it was also offered to the Communist world as a general objective toward which all would strive.

At the Twenty-second Party Congress each fraternal party delegate solemnly rose and paid tribute to the Soviet program. After the Congress, at many plenary sessions of parties loyal to Moscow, parallel programs incorporating the general outlines of the Moscow path-to-Communism were approved.

But Peking did not approve. Why?

A Western diplomat offered me a cogent explanation. He had just come back from a three weeks' trip through China.

"You will not find anyone starving in China," he said. "But they are living on the equivalent of about fifteen dollars a month. The single men and women live in barracks. There may or may not be a room for married couples. Sometimes, they are allowed a room to themselves only one night a week. A meal costs about fifteen cents. Rice and a little cabbage is the diet. This is austerity. They work long, long hours. Working conditions are bad."

In these conditions, he felt, it was inconceivable that any Chinese government could give publicity to the consumer-oriented Soviet Communist goals with their emphasis on short work hours, long vacations, private apartments, a big rise in the standard of living.

"It would make a mockery of the life the Chinese live under Communism," he said. "And it is obvious there will be no great improvement for a long time to come."

An East European Communist stated the point in slightly

different fashion. He noted that the Chinese had long insisted on describing the Communist world as "the great camp of Communist powers, headed by the Soviet Union." There had been a sharp dispute over this phraseology at the 1957 Communist meeting in Moscow. The Russians opposed being placed at the "head" of the "camp."

"This was not an esoteric argument," the East European told me.

What was involved was a most important analogy. The Chinese, in effect, were submitting themselves to the leadership of the Soviet "head." But in return they expected to be treated as an equalitarian element in the "camp." This implied that whatever resources the "camp of Communism" possessed would be shared as an army shares its rations of food and munitions. Russia, as the leader, might have certain special privileges. But China, as a loyal follower, was entitled to a fair share of whatever goods and supplies were available.

But the Russians had violated this concept. The violations had been consistent and constant. The chiefs of the Chinese Army had never been able to obtain from their Soviet Army counterparts the most modern weapons available. They had not been able to get rocket weapons, advanced types of aircraft, missiles and, of course, they had not been given nuclear weapons.

The Soviet Union had insisted on sharing such surpluses as were available not only within the Communist "camp" but entirely outside it. She gave material aid to a whole string of Asian and African client countries with nationalist regimes, including a number of states which were monarchies and some states where the Communists were outlawed and hounded almost to extinction.

Perhaps the most notable example of Khrushchev's unwillingness to "share and share alike" with China had occurred in the course of his 1960 trip to Southeast Asia. Not only had he expressed sympathy for India in her deepening quarrel with China; he had pledged to Indonesia some $200 or $300 million in aid which China had expected—and badly needed. And he had done this at a moment when China and Indonesia were quarreling bitterly over the role of the overseas Chinese in the Indonesian islands.

Viewed in this perspective, small wonder that the two movements had drifted further and further apart. They simply did not see the world from the same perspective. The Chinese insisted that the balance of power had shifted to the Communist side and, hence, that the time was ripe for a crushing revolutionary offensive to wipe out the last vestiges of colonialism and imperialism. America, they said (apparently believing their own propaganda), was a paper tiger. The Chinese were confident of their ability to survive any nuclear war. In fact, a revolutionary offensive which would turn Asia, Africa and Latin America into flaming caldrons would greatly ease China's internal conflicts and permit her to inherit supreme power on the Asian continent. This was never mentioned but it was not likely to escape the Kremlin strategists.

Moscow put its side with frankness. It was all very well to call for world revolution and liberation of colonial masses. But if nuclear war was touched off there would be nothing left to liberate. The world would go up in one great explosion. Again and again and again Moscow hammered at China that No. 1 priority must be given to maintenance of peace because the alternative was the destruction of the world.

As the conflict wore on, the language displayed more and more asperity. The Russians made slightly veiled references to the resemblance between China's views and the theory of "permanent revolution" of the anathematized Trotsky. From the Chinese came suggestions that Khrushchev was a "revisionist" and little better than Karl Kautsky, the famous Socialist whom Lenin had branded a "renegade" to Marxism.

Cultural contacts between Moscow and Peking began to dry up. Chinese films disappeared from Russian houses. Translations of Chinese works vanished from the Soviet journals. Chinese books could not be found in Soviet bookstores. Chinese broadcasts were dropped from the Moscow radio. And soon the parties began to broadcast to each other by short-wave radio—and to jam each other's broadcasts, just as, for years, they had jammed the broadcasts of the Voice of America.

But, perhaps, the clearest insight into what the Russians saw ahead in the field of relations with China was provided by the assignment of Major General Alexander S. Panyushkin to handle relations between the Central Committee of the Soviet Communist party and the Chinese party. Panyushkin was one of the top specialists in Soviet intelligence. For many years he was chief of the Second Section of the Committee on State Security—that entrusted with foreign intelligence. He was trained as an army officer but had carried on intelligence functions for many years. He served as Soviet Ambassador to the Chiang Kai-shek regime in Chungking from 1939 to 1944. After a brief interlude he was assigned as Ambassador to Washington. He returned in 1950 to Moscow and was again assigned to China in 1952—this time to the Communist regime. One of the first acts of the post-Stalin regime was to withdraw Panyushkin from Peking. He was recalled March 10, 1953—only five days after the death of Stalin.

The move was taken in an effort to improve relations between the two countries. Panyushkin was *persona non grata* with Mao Tse-tung, and his appointment had been regarded as an open provocation on the part of Stalin.

Relations between the Moscow party and Peking had been handled largely by Mikhail A. Suslov for several years. He had been entrusted with the delicate task presumably because of the Stalinist orientation of his ideology, which made it easier for him to maintain personal relations with the Chinese leaders.

To shift the conduct of party relations from Suslov to Panyushkin was simply to affront the Chinese in the most blatant manner, putting them on notice that from the Soviet side relations henceforth would be governed not by comradely considerations but by the requirements of military intelligence.

The step was taken, nonetheless, in the winter of 1962 and marked the practical abandonment of pretense from the Moscow side that the quarrel was negotiable. Swiftly thereafter reports began to seep out of China of private party briefings in which the Chinese sought to place major blame on Moscow for many of their economic, social and political difficulties.

Nevertheless, there were signs that each side hoped to hold the line just short of a complete break. This would enable them to preserve the military clauses of the 1950 Defense Alliance which obligate each state to come to the defense of the other under most conditions of attack.

Moscow would continue to back (however lukewarmly) China's right to membership in the United Nations and her claim to the island of Formosa. Diplomatic relations would be preserved. Cultural relations would continue on a minimum basis (somewhat less than the level of exchanges between the U. S. A. and the U. S. S. R.). Party contacts would be confined to an arm's-length relationship, somewhat similar to that between the Yugoslav and Russian parties.

The ability of Moscow and Peking to maintain so precarious a balance in their relationship while at the same time vigorously competing for influence and prestige both among the Communist movements of the world and among the emerging nationalist and nascent colonial states was open to grave doubt.

There was every sign by the spring of 1962 that—unless new external pressures in the shape of a crisis in relations with the West should emerge—the two Communist world powers would move steadily forward to greater alienation with all the complex consequences which inevitably would arise.

9. A Nation in Flux

In the winter of 1962 I could pick up the telephone in my room at the Hotel National, ask for my office in London or New York, receive the call within a few minutes, dictate whatever commentary I wished and hang up. There was no censorship, no bar on what kind of dispatch I transmitted. For the first time since the days just after the Bolshevik Revolution (except for an interlude of a few weeks late in 1945) the Soviet censorship on foreign correspondence had ceased to exist in the spring of 1961.

For the first time in Soviet history direct teletype circuits were being set up between the Moscow offices of foreign newsmen and their European bureaus. The State Secrets Act which forbade Soviet citizens to give information to foreign correspondents had not been repealed but it was no longer observed. This did not mean that I could telephone Mr. Khrushchev's office in the Kremlin and get an appointment. But it did mean I could call *Pravda's* Information Bureau and check the text of the remarks the Premier had made in a speech to farmers in Novosibirsk last year.

But there was a curiously uneven quality about all this. The Press Department of the Foreign Office could and did call in correspondents and upbraid them for the most unlikely offenses. One man was lectured severely for publishing a book he had written before coming to the Soviet Union. A colleague on the *New York Times* was reprimanded because the Press Department felt the articles I published on my return from Moscow in February, 1962, were "very bad" and "anti-Soviet."

The new dispensation did not prevent Soviet authorities from expelling correspondents, sometimes on charges of espionage (as in the case of two Germans) and sometimes in reprisal for editorials in their newspapers (as in the case of a man with *Le Monde*). Nor did it prevent them from attempting to carry out the vilest kind of provocations, using police undercover agents, knockout drops, compromising photographs and the traditional apparatus of blackmail.

The new and the old persisted side by side and this was characteristic of the present state of Soviet evolution.

Driving in from the fine Sheremetov International Airport the eye was struck by a highway clover-leaf, the first installation of its kind in Russia's still primitive road system. Within the city the character of the once beautiful Sadovo or Garden ring around the old "white" city was in the process of complete change. Through the construction of underpasses and pedestrian tunnels it was becoming Moscow's first limited-access freeway.

But there was no corresponding boost in private automobile ownership. Indeed, passenger car production continued to be held at the low level of about 150,000 units a year. Premier Khrushchev insisted that Russia would not go in for mass usage of private cars like America. Public transport and taxis would be the backbone of the system.

Few Khrushchev decisions were less in line with public demand. To the Russian as to the American the car was the symbol of better living and Russians made no secret of their desire for automobiles, whatever the party might say.

Not that public transport was working well. Moscow was in the throes of its worst taxi shortage since World War II. The papers were filled with complaints. A half-hour wait in a taxi queue was average. Jitney routes had been set up —limousines plying well-traveled routes. And government chauffeurs did big business after hours with black market taxi service, using government cars and government gasoline. The trouble was simple. The government would not give the Moscow Taxi Trust enough cars to meet the city's big growth and the Trust would not pay overtime to drivers to handle the rush-hour crowds.

Fancy store fronts—and stores—had blossomed all over the city. Window displays had taken on a vaguely Parisian cast. (Moscow retail stores purchased the stock of modernistic mannequins, models and display materials brought in by the French for the 1961 Exposition. The effect on Gorky Street and other shopping centers was striking.) Not all the new stores served consumer purposes. For instance, the big neon-lighted "Isotope" store on the route from the airport to Moscow was designed to impress foreigners with the Soviet surplus of radioactive isotopes.

The pent-up passion of Moscow men and women for pretty, pleasant Western fripperies was demonstrated when the Beriozka (Birch Tree) chain opened a beautiful modernistic establishment on Gorky street, next door to the old Lux Hotel, once the mysterious haunt of Comintern agents. The store was stocked with foreign goods—brass vases from India, sparkling Czech crystal, porcelain nude figurines (a rarity for prudish Moscow), and counters laden with tasteful (and cheap) Western costume jewelry. Such crowds stormed the establishment that traffic was hindered and the police had to set up barricades.

One Sunday I went to the great Central Moscow Market. I knew that meat had been scarce for months. A few days before I had seen a block-long queue on Gorky Street outside the big sausage store. Many Moscow residents had been sending meat packages to friends and relatives in the provinces where supplies were even shorter—although this was technically against the law. In the music halls there were bitter jokes about farmers coming to town to buy food.

As I walked from counter to counter looking at the ragged-looking veal, selling for $1.50 a pound, stew meat for $1 and bacon fat at $1.50, I noticed a woman just ahead of me, doing the same thing. She was dressed in black, carried a string bag, or *avoska* (*avos* means "perhaps" or "maybe"), and appeared to be in her late sixties. As she wandered from counter to counter I heard her mutter again and again: *"Kashmar!* A nightmare! *Kak mozhno zhit?* How can one live?"

She was not the only one who was asking this question. A taxi driver after questioning me about the pay of cabmen in America said bitterly: "And I earn seventy rubles [about $77] a month! Can you live on that? The devil knows you can't!"

Russia's bread was as good, as cheap, as abundant as ever. Even vegetables and fruit were in fairly good supply, although the Chinese apples which graced the Russian markets for several years were no longer to be had.

But meat, milk and eggs were scarce. Eggs vanished from the government stores whenever a holiday was approaching and hardly appeared all winter long when the Russian hens almost halt laying. In the peasant market eggs sold at nearly $3 a dozen. Milk supplies were erratic. Some days there would be deliveries. Then there would be none for a whole week.

The most productive source of meat, milk, eggs—as well as fruit and vegetables—was the individual peasant garden plot and the intensively cultivated gardens of the dacha owners in the suburban areas of cities like Moscow. Yet, while Premier Khrushchev was insisting on greater profit incentive for the peasants so as to boost their output, party propagandists were cracking down on private production. Dacha owners were being intimidated from selling their eggs, milk or apples (on grounds this was small-scale capitalism) and when peasants managed to increase their flocks of chickens or litters of pigs they were promptly compelled to sell them to the collective or state farm.

Perhaps it was contradictions of this kind which gave rise to a bumper crop of political and satirical stories. Never in my years in Moscow had I heard so many. Many of these jokes were set in the framework of an imaginary question-and-answer program on the Armenian radio.

For example:

QUESTION: Given the conditions of France is it possible to construct Communism there?

ANSWER: Yes. But why should they?

Or:

QUESTION: Why has the Armenian radio stopped answering questions?

ANSWER: Because the old Jew who wrote them has died.

Or:

QUESTION: What nationality were Adam and Eve?

ANSWER: Russian.

QUESTION: How do you know?

ANSWER: Because they were both naked, had only an apple

to eat and thought they were in paradise!

Or, on a nonpolitical theme:

QUESTION: I am an eighteen-year-old girl. What time should I go to bed?

ANSWER: You should be in bed by ten o'clock so you can be home by midnight.

QUESTION: I am an eighteen-year-old girl. Last night I stayed out until 2 A.M. Did I do wrong?

ANSWER: Try and remember.

Not all the jokes were so lighthearted. A favorite dealt with a new five-story building. When finished it was discovered that by mistake no toilets had been installed. What to do with the structure? The solution required some ingenuity. The ground floor offered no problem. It was turned over to stores. No toilets were needed there. The second floor was given to a kindergarten. No toilets were needed because the children all wore diapers. The third floor was given to ordinary workers for apartments. They would have to run up and down three stories but they were so used to inconvenience they would not mind one more hardship. The fourth floor was given to pensioners. They were aged and used to using chamberpots anyway. The fifth floor was given to the bosses on the theory they could use the windows. If someone happened to be below it made no difference. The bosses were accustomed to relieving themselves at the workers' cost.

It was not only in such harsh and savage satire that Russians revealed revulsion against the style and trappings of the regime they had so long endured. The same mood was expressed in chance remarks. The contemptuous epithet of a cab driver to a workman who held up his passage along the street: "*Vot rabochi klass!* There's the working class for you!" Or the working-class woman who sputtered at me one day as I walked through an underpass in the subway: *"Brrr . . . Kommunism! Brrr . . . Kommunism!"* And then spat demonstratively and strode away.

Russia was losing—at least temporarily—the iron, regimented character which had so long been its most notable feature. Moscow was becoming a city of gossip and tittle-tattle, of rumor and talebearing. It was more of a "court" city than it had been since the capital was removed to St. Petersburg by Peter the Great. With the new intermingling of foreign diplomats and Russians the embassies now often found themselves in possession of so many different versions of a given rumor that it was impossible to know which might be true.

After the Twenty-second Party Congress no less than three different rumors of important suicides were circulated. None of them turned out to be correct, although there were persons who remained convinced that Mme. Furtseva did attempt to take her life in despair at being dropped without notice from the party Presidium. She certainly was ill and in the hospital, but whether or not she took an overdose of sleeping pills after being upbraided by her deputy, Mr. Kuznetsov, for failing to "act like a Communist" may never be known. For two or three weeks all Moscow gabbled about Mme. Furtseva, how she collapsed under Kuznetsov's assault, how he took her name down from the door at the Ministry of Culture and put his own up, how she wrote an apology to Premier Khrushchev, how she waited and waited for an answer, which finally came in the form of a bouquet of roses from the Presidium, and how she then rose triumphantly from her hospital bed and returned to the Ministry (where her name had been hastily repainted on the door) and how all those persons, headed by Kuznetsov, who had traded on her disgrace now were quivering in their boots.

The rumors about Nuritdin Mukhitdinov and old Marshal Voroshilov were not elaborated in such detail. Mukhitdinov was said to have shot himself because of losing his Presidium place. The report was not true. Several weeks later he turned up in a minor government post. Nor did Voroshilov commit suicide. He suffered severe public humiliation, notably at the Twenty-second Party Congress and at the November 7 Red Square parade when he was barred from taking his usual place on the Mausoleum. But at the Kremlin New Year's Eve reception he was publicly bussed by Mr. Khruschev and permitted to drink a toast with Anastas Mikoyan. He kept his seat in the Supreme Soviet while Mme. Furtseva and Mukhitdinov were losing theirs.

But it was just this freedom with which rumors circulated in Moscow which gave apparent credibility in the West to the reports about former Foreign Minister Molotov. Interest was aroused when Molotov returned to Moscow from Vienna for the Twenty-second Party Congress. It was heightened by the attacks upon him and the revelations that he had been writing critical commentaries to the Central Committee and to the party journal, *Kommunist*.

When it was then reported after the Congress that he was returning to his Vienna post; when it appeared that the violent demands expressed at the Twenty-second Party Congress for his expulsion from the party were being ignored; when he did not, in fact, reappear in Vienna; the wildest kind of speculation arose in the West. A new struggle for power had risen in Moscow. Khrushchev and Molotov were vying for favor. The Central Committee had been summoned to the Kremlin and was in continuous session.

The Molotov situation was not without political significance but most of the headlines stemmed from the blunders of two or three clerks in the Foreign Office. It was an underling in the Press Department, trying to be helpful, who told a correspondent, in response to a query, that Molotov was going back to Vienna. The information happened to be wrong but, in keeping with the tradition of Soviet bureaucracy, once the mistake had been made no official would frankly admit this fact. So the rumors continued to build up.

One crisp January day when Western newspapers were filled with stories about the "crisis" in the Kremlin I wandered over to see what was actually happening within the rose-walled, half-mile-square compound which is the heart of Moscow. The sky was blue and the Kremlin churches sparkled in their fresh gilt. There were throngs of sight-seers inspecting the modernistic new Kremlin Palace of Soviets with its Park Avenue architecture, escalators and fine expanses of glass-and-marble walls. The souvenir shops in the great Cathedral Square were doing a brisk business in "Kremlin" scarfs ($5) and picture postcards. The Taininsky or "Secret" Garden along the Moskva River side of the enclosure was swarming with youngsters, sliding down the great ice Russian bear, feature of the continuous holiday party which brought more than 100,000 children into the Kremlin in the first fortnight of January. Wherever I looked there were children, their parents and tourists from out of town. Loudspeakers were blaring forth circus music and announcements about lost children.

If there had been a "secret" meeting of the Central Committee under way to cope with the Molotov affair it would have had a hard time hearing itself think over the hubbub and gaiety. But, as I well knew, no such meeting was in progress. Khrushchev was off on another of his endless farm tours and was heading for a hunting holiday in the Carpatho-Ukrainian mountains. Most of the other Presidium members were out of town. Moscow had seldom presented an aspect more quiet and normal. The only bit of gossip about Molotov which I knew to be a fact was that the Molotovs had let go one of their three maids recently—but not in anticipation of trouble. Simply because she had been nipping bottles out of the wine cellar.

It seemed to me that, in a sense, this story of the Molotov maid told more about the state of Russia today than most of the others. The Revolution had slipped a long way into the past when a servant was fired for stealing from the wine cellar of a man who had been one of its fiery young ascetics. How many wine cellars, I wondered, might there now be in Moscow and how many servants were there in the households of the present leaders of the Bolsheviki?

I did not know whether, in the end, the party would find it necessary or advisable to take away from Mr. Molotov the membership card which he had held since 1906. But I was sure that even in such an event he would be permitted to enjoy the pleasures of his wine cellar with no greater harassments than those stemming from a dishonest servant girl. The penalties of political controversy in Russia might still be more severe than in the West. But they had changed since 1952, when Mr. Molotov, among the most loyal of Stalin's followers, was viewed with such suspicion in the Kremlin that his wife was sent to Siberia and he himself was being measured for a victim's role in a forthcoming purge trial.

That Russia was a nation in flux today was no longer to be doubted. Would the direction of the flux be to the West or to the East, to the new or to the old, back toward Stalin or ahead beyond Khrushchev? This was the heart of the matter.

10. Whither Russia?

For a hundred years the question had been asked again and again in Russia—whither the future? Throughout the nineteenth century it was debated between Slavophile and Westernizer, between Moscow and Petersburg, between Anarchist and Marxist, between Mensheviki and Bolsheviki. Herzen demanded: Who Is Guilty? Chernyshevsky demanded: What Is to Be Done? Dostoyevsky asked where the Russian troika was bound, thundering across the mysterious earth.

And today in Moscow I found the question being asked once more. Here was evidence of the validity of George Kennan's thesis of the continuity in the main stream of Russian culture, of the persistence and vigorous growth into the present era of the liberal tradition of the pre-Bolshevik epoch. Was this the most powerful tendency in Russian society? Would it, as Kennan postulated, gradually overcome and vanquish the authoritarian retrogression which had come about, almost by chance, through the accidental triumph of

Bolshevism in 1917 and its evolution into Stalinism?

I felt confident that Russia's intelligentsia and a sub-
stantial majority of Soviet citizens shared this hope. Khrushchev might act to the contrary but liberalism was what he
kept promising the people. The continuation of liberalization
was implied in the new reign of law; in the vigorous assaults
on Stalin; in the rehabilitation of his victims; in the liquida-
tion of the police state; in the democratization of the Communist party incorporated in its new statute; in what was
known of the general outlines of the new Soviet Constitution
which Khrushchev was drafting as a monument to his regime
in place of the Constitution which Bukharin had drawn up
for Stalin.

To many young Russians it seemed that a new day was
dawning. They were angry when foreigners reminded them
of ills committed under Stalin.

"We had nothing to do with that," they said. "If you only
knew how much blood he cost us. We have repudiated Stalin.
We are done with him. This is a new regime. Why do we
have to be reminded of what is past?"

They were shocked when an outspoken American said,
"For years Russia was run by a gangster, part madman, part
criminal. We knew this and we told you about it. You did not
believe us. It was not easy living in the world with your
country while Stalin ran it. We hope we never have to again.
But don't blame us if we remember the past and still treat
you with caution."

Not that the foreigners in Moscow underestimated the
change in atmosphere. They valued their new Russian
friends. They accepted as sincere remarks by Russians who
expressed relief and approval of the strong anti-Stalin line
of the Twenty-second Party Congress.

"The great difference in Moscow today as compared with

two or three years ago," one diplomat said, "is in spirit. In spite of the war tension last fall the Russians have not panicked. They have not become American-haters. They do not insult Americans. They do not assault the American exhibitions."

My experience bore this out. I encountered questions and sometimes hard arguments. But not hatred or anger. And often I heard: "It is not America we fear—it is Germany."

I heard diplomats talking about the "democratization of Soviet rule," and if this seemed to me to be slightly premature, I conceded that the regime was trying bold innovations like the interview which President Kennedy gave to Alexei Adzhubei. This was an experiment in unshackling Russian minds, in permitting Soviet citizens to read a reasoned statement of the American position. I found Russians poring over the Kennedy text in deep Siberia and even in Outer Mongolia. I watched them read it on the day of publication, standing in wind and snow before the street bulletin boards for fifteen or twenty minutes, absorbing every word of a full page of type.

This was bound to create areas of shadow and doubt in Russian minds. It was a new "thaw," a more profound one than that of the immediate post-Stalin years. Perhaps it might be compared with that of the 1860's after Alexander II freed the serfs and (temporarily) abandoned the censorship. The regime was deliberately encouraging a spirit of free inquiry. It did not always like the results—as could be seen in the way it treated creative artists—but it was the regime itself which provided the opportunity for original thought. The momentum was powerful and steady. Was it irresistible? I did not think so. It depended very much upon one man, Nikita Sergeivich Khrushchev. He was sixty-eight years old. His health was good but he suffered from high blood pressure. He was a man of enormous energy but, more often, he had to recuperate from tremendous outbursts of activity with long vacations at Sochi or Yalta. He was careful of his low-salt diet in public and took only a glass or two of white wine on state occasions. But, privately, he sometimes broke the rules. For relaxation he liked to hunt, take steam baths (he had a private *sauna,* built for him by the Finnish government at his country house outside Moscow) or swim in the Black Sea with the aid of water wings, never having learned to swim during his boyhood in the coal mines. For some years Khrushchev might hold the helm, but what lay beyond?

This was the most difficult question to assess. Within the Presidium there was now a "troika"—a three-way balance between older men who could be counted upon to follow ideas similar to Khrushchev's; middle men of bland bureaucratic personality like Frol Kozlov; and Young Turks, untested, vigorous, ambitious. Khrushchev was supreme. He ruled all three groups. He had eliminated most of the "collective leaders" who originally made up the Presidium. The June, 1957, revolt in which he was confronted with a two-thirds majority against him had decided the fate of Malenkov, Molotov, Kaganovich, Shepilov, Saburov, Pervukhin, Bulganin and Voroshilov. Marshal Zhukov and Mr. Khrushchev's old Ukrainian associate, Kirichenko, had been dropped by the wayside. The attrition continued at the Twenty-second Party Congress with the loss of Aristov, Ignatov, Mukhitdinov and Furtseva. Two continuing members, Otto Kuusinen and Nikolai Shvernik, were superannuated. Presumably they were kept on to provide Khrushchev with two pocket votes.

The older group comprised five men—Khrushchev, Mikoyan, Suslov, Kuusinen and Shvernik. The middle group included Kozlov, who had been formally designated by

Khrushchev as his successor and whose name was given a special out-of-alphabetic order position in the listing, Leonid Brezhnev and Alexei Kosygin.

The middle men were more notable as doers than thinkers. Despite his role as heir apparent Kozlov was not given a chance of lasting out the first round after Khrushchev's death. Both Kosygin and Brezhnev were rated his superiors in ability. Some observers thought Khrushchev had deliberately named Kozlov as his heir because there was little chance of Kozlov developing independent political power.

The real strength of the Presidium lay in its younger members—Podgorny, Poliansky, Voronov and the candidate member, Shcherbitzky. Equally important were the new members of the Secretariat, Pyotr Demichev, Leonid Ilyichev and Alexander Shelepin. These were the Young Turks. For the most part they were men in their forties, able, aggressive men. Not too much was known of their ideological leanings. Perhaps they themselves would not know which direction they were moving in until the time for the move came.

Among the older men there was one enigma—Suslov. He had served Stalin faithfully as an ideologue. He had performed the same chore for Khrushchev. Was he the fanatic zealot whom many in Moscow supposed him to be? Did he secretly yearn for China's hard line? He had supported Khrushchev in the infighting of June, 1957, and had been given responsibility for relations with China which now had come to the breaking point.

Many persons in Moscow saw him as a sinister figure, the *eminence grise* behind the rise of neo-Stalinists like Ilyichev, the quiet sponsor of a coterie of powerful younger men, particularly in the press and propaganda field.

There was another grouping of young-men-in-a-hurry. The best known among them was Khrushchev's son-in-law,

Adzhubei, a ruthless, clever manipulator who floated trial balloons for his father-in-law and engaged the Premier in rough-and-ready argument in the style which characterized the Khrushchev family circle. In that circle no holds were barred and the decisive voice was often that of Nina Petrovna, the Premier's motherly wife, full of good sense, quiet and determined.

Adzhubei was a controversial figure in Soviet society. There were not a few important men who made no secret of their dislike for him. They criticized his flashy innovations in *Izvestia* and said he had committed a disservice to his country by trying to interview and argue with President Kennedy at the same time, doing rather badly at both.

But Adzhubei had connections—in addition to his father-in-law. He was close to Shelepin. When Shelepin was head of the Young Communist movement Adzhubei was editor of the Young Communist newspaper. They worked together. When Shelepin was named head of the Committee on State Security Adzhubei was editor of *Izvestia*. They continued to work together. When Shelepin joined the party Secretariat his successor in the Young Communist movement, Semichastny, took over the state security job. The three men, plus Pavlov, who succeeded Semichastny as head of the Youth movement, formed a political nucleus. Shelepin was said to have "defused" the security apparatus, eliminating its political potential and correcting the many Stalin-Beria injustices. Not everyone in Moscow was convinced that the secret police had for all time been removed as a political factor. In a showdown some wondered whether the Adzhubei-Shelepin clique might not be able to wield this weapon.

Adzhubei seemed to follow a double-gaited line. *Izvestia* was open both to liberal viewpoints and to neo-Stalinists. His associates, however, were among the most hard-nosed of the neo-Stalinists. Semichastny and Pavlov actively preached violence against nonconformists. They had no qualms about riding roughshod over the new legal reforms. It was this group which backed use of the death penalty to terrorize collective farmers who didn't look after their machinery and bookkeepers who cooked the government's accounts. They stirred up campaigns against the churches, inveighed against private garden plots and personal automobiles, denounced abstract painters as parasites and terrorized innocent young couples who danced in Western style at the cafés. If power fell in the hands of these ambitious men of no principle there would be trouble ahead for Russian men of goodwill.

There was no easy formula for the transfer of political power in Russia. The electoral system was merely a device for registering the popularity of the regime. There was neither mechanism nor tradition for a succession to the leadership except by the murderous method of the struggle for power which had produced, first, a Stalin and, nearly thirty years later, a Khrushchev. There were hints that the new Khrushchev Constitution might seek to correct this situation by introducing at least the first steps toward political democracy of the elective type. There were hints that distinctions between party and nonparty no longer were important. But these were only hints and Khrushchev would hardly live long enough for so fundamental a change to take deep roots.

This meant that the Soviet apparatus, manipulation of the police, the army, the Central Committee, the ministerial organizations, could once again play a major role.

What was the inner politics of the present situation? Within the party there were deep undercurrents of unknown strength set in motion by the Soviet-Chinese conflict. The competition of rival viewpoints had been reproduced in concealed form within the Societ party. Khrushchev had won the day but his opponents had not been driven out of the party. Some had adopted the protective coloration of neo-Stalinism. Some had taken refuge in silence. But they were still there. Khrushchev had no fear of Molotov and the older generation. He had broken Malenkov over the Leningrad affair and Malenkov's complicity with Beria in the party purges. But there were elements inside the party who could make trouble. Even those who backed Khrushchev were not happy over the break with China and the divisive split which had weakened the world movement. Khrushchev had other secret opponents. There were those who criticized his failure to solve the agricultural problem. It was no accident that Khrushchev spent so much time exhorting the farmers. He knew this was his Achilles' heel. Unless he got big boosts in food production he could not meet his industrial goals and his promises of a higher standard of living. His diplomacy was cramped by lack of supplies to deliver to client countries.

Nor was it certain that Khrushchev's new tactic, the abandonment of Russia's three-field crop rotation system, would give the results he needed. It would require almost double the 22 million metric tons of fertilizer now available and there was no chance of closing the gap for years.

He had dismissed some of his ablest farm advisers—men like Matzkevich and Shevchenko—relying increasingly on the sinister but pragmatic Trofim Lysenko, who had come close to destroying Soviet biology and agronomy under Stalin. But in April, 1962, Lysenko's health broke and he was compelled to retire once more.

If Khrushchev suffered new agricultural setbacks the consequences might be far-reaching.

The army, which played an important role during the ascendency of Marshal Zhukov and the drive to crush the secret police, was quiescent. Khrushchev had cleverly maneuvered the marshals and set them against each other. But there were smoldering embers of ill will, particularly among the officers who had been released in Khrushchev's big cutbacks of military personnel. Many of them, working in Siberian industry and Kazakstan state farms, grumbled openly about the regime. The General Staff was nervous about Khrushchev's inability to achieve a genuine relaxation of tensions. They felt they had put Russia ahead of the United States in military capability but did not know how long they could maintain the edge. It was up to Khrushchev to cash in quickly on the opportunity which they had given him.

There were men on the Western side who also felt that time was running out.

"The year 1962 is the year of decision," said one diplomat with many years of service in Moscow. "We must negotiate with Khrushchev before he gets boxed in. His problem with China is very serious. We cannot count on his patience indefinitely."

This man felt that a German peace treaty was more important to Khrushchev than Berlin and a disarmament treaty more important than anything else. He did not see an easy solution to any of these questions. He saw no chance whatever without a meeting of Khrushchev and Kennedy and probably of Khrushchev and Adenauer. Another Western observer felt that despite the lack of ground for maneuver the logic of events was pushing Russia and the West toward a resolution of their most acute differences. He admitted that the Soviet obduracy on the Western demand for inspection posed the most difficult of barriers, but he did not believe Khrushchev's refusal to permit inspection was deliberately designed to prevent agreement.

"Rightly or wrongly, the Russians feel that secrecy is a major military asset," he said. "Perhaps they believe we do not know the location of their missile-launch sites. If so this would give them an edge in nuclear war—since American sites are known. Perhaps inspection might disclose unexpected Soviet military weaknesses."

Either way this observer felt that Khrushchev regarded secrecy as one of the most valued cards in his hand. He would not play it until late in the game and only when the United States was ready to play a card of equally high value.

"I am an optimist," one Russian close to the Soviet hierarchy told me. "My government knows that nuclear war means the end of the world. Your leaders know this too. Of course, it is difficult. But we have no alternative except to find a way to agreement."

But I could not escape a sense of deep urgency. As one diplomat said, "We must settle things now. It is too dangerous. Too many unexpected things might occur. Khrushchev is not eternal. He is strong but not all-powerful. Suppose he died tomorrow—then where would we be?"

Or as an important Soviet official said, "The big difficulty now is prestige. Your prestige and ours. Somehow we must create an atmosphere in which a solution is possible."

A man who spent many years in the world of international Communism said, "I feel a little edgy. The Molotov thing didn't mean anything. Khrushchev is strong enough to handle the Chinese—and yet he was defied by the Albanians. That is the sort of thing which means something on the inside. Until the summer of 1961 I don't think any of the European Communists really thought there *could* be another war. Now they are not so sure. Everyone would feel better if Khrushchev and Kennedy could get together."

So it seemed to me. If peace could be preserved and strengthened; if the longed-for *détente* of Russia and the West could be achieved; then the forces for liberalization of

Russia would be strengthened. The evolution would go forward. The balance would tip strongly in the direction of the West. The momentum toward democratization of the Soviet regime would gather speed. The hopes of the Russian intelligentsia would be realized—and the world would be made safer to live in.

But if the great powers failed to solve their difficulties; if tension rose; if the Chinese view of the world was confirmed; if Khrushchev's foreign policy again proved barren; if his domestic problems piled higher; then the neo-Stalinists and the bullyboys would have their chance. They would have to wait for the death of Khrushchev and even then it would be a fight. The odds would favor their success.

America's stake in Russia's future was great. On this hung the great questions—peace or war, survival or disaster. We could not predict who would succeed Khrushchev. We could not be certain which course Russia would take. But it was obvious which direction would be best for the world and we were not without influence. Our decisions as well as those of Khrushchev would determine the international climate. Our diplomacy and posture played a role in Russia's internal dilemma. We knew Khrushchev as a difficult man and Russia as a difficult neighbor. Yet it was not hard to imagine a worse combination—a Russia and China guided by Mao Tse-tung's implacable revolutionary dogma, for example. Might we so conduct our relations with Moscow that the question mark could be removed and the phrase written not as "A New Russia?" but as "A New Russia"?

If this could be done, it was worth doing. Russian liberalism was a hardy plant. It had survived a hundred years of oppression under the Czars. It had lived through a bloody Revolution and more than a quarter of a century of Stalinism. The ferment of change was working in every sensitive sector of Russian life. It was influencing Russia's relations with both East and West and, more vitally, the relations of Russians with Russians. The only significant and lasting change in Russia must come from within. The reaction against tyranny must be that of the Russian people. Given a reasonable chance the flower of change could still blossom on the wind-swept steppe. In a thermonuclear age this might be a salvation.

Index

Index

About the Author

A writer since his college days at the University of Minnesota, and long considered one of the *New York Times*'s most respected journalists, Harrison E. Salisbury probably knows Russia better than any living American correspondent. He has devoted over eighteen years of his life to studying Russia, speaks the language, has lived there as a resident correspondent for many years, and has traveled widely through almost every part of the Soviet Union, including the long-sealed-off regions of Siberia, the sub-Arctic and Central Asia, as well as the Volga country and the Ukraine.

Mr. Salisbury's first assignment in Russia was as head of the UP bureau in Moscow in 1944. At this time he spent eight months in wartime Russia, and traveled about 25,000 miles, visiting the fronts and liberated cities.

Following a three-year period as Foreign News Editor of the UP, Mr. Salisbury joined the *New York Times* in 1949. He was again sent to Russia as Moscow correspondent and remained there for the next five years. Out of his observations of the Russia of this period grew his celebrated series of articles for the *New York Times*, "Russia Re-Viewed," which brought him the Pulitzer Prize for international correspondence in 1955. His two books dealing with the same period followed, *American in Russia* (1955) and *Moscow Journal—The End of Stalin* (1961).

Because the Soviet authorities objected to his reports both in the prize-winning series and in *American in Russia*, Mr. Salisbury was subsequently barred from Russia for five years. During this time he worked as a reporter on the city staff of the *Times* and wrote some notable series on such domestic issues as urban transportation and juvenile delinquency. The latter was expanded into the book *The Shook-up Generation* (1958).

It was not until the spring of 1959, when the restrictions of the Cold War were temporarily lifted, that Mr. Salisbury was allowed to revisit Russia and personally observe and evaluate the changes between Khrushchev's and Stalin's regimes. For more than a year he again traveled thousands of miles within the Soviet Union, visiting Siberia twice and making an extended stay in Mongolia, which offered him a unique opportunity for examining Soviet-Chinese relations. He wrote *To Moscow—and Beyond* (1960) to report on this trip.

Mr. Salisbury's present book, *A New Russia?*, was written on his return from his sixth and most recent visit to Russia, which he made in the late fall of 1961 after traveling through the ancient lands of Iran and Afghanistan on another *Times* assignment.

Since his return from Russia in February of 1962, Harrison Salisbury has been appointed Director of National Correspondence for the *New York Times*. Besides his five nonfiction books about Russia, Mr. Salisbury has also written a novel, *The Northern Palmyra Affair* (1962), about the city of Leningrad and its citizens, for which he has a special and deep affection. The book was a Literary Guild Selection and has received wide acclaim.

Set in Linotype Baskerville
Format by Sidney Feinberg
Manufactured by The Haddon Craftsmen, Inc.
HARPER & ROW, PUBLISHERS, *New York and Evanston*